Common Core Literacy Lesson Plans

Ready-to-Use Resources, 9–12

EYE ON EDUCATION

Eye On Education
6 Depot Way West, Suite 106
Larchmont, NY 10538
(914) 833-0551
(914) 833-0761 Fax
www.eyeoneducation.com

Library of Congress Cataloging-in-Publication Data

Common core literacy lesson plans : ready-to-use resources, 9–12.
       p.   cm.
Includes bibliographical references.
ISBN 978-1-59667-225-3
1. Language arts (Secondary)—Curricula—United States.
2. Language arts (Secondary)—Standards—United States.
I. Eye on Education (Firm)
LB1631.C658 2012
428.0071′2—dc23   2012025664

Contributing Writer: Lesli J. Favor, PhD
Sponsoring Editor: Robert Sickles
Production Editor: Lauren Davis
Copy Editor: Kathleen White
Designer and Compositor: Matthew Williams, click! Publishing Services
Cover Designer: Dave Strauss, 3FoldDesign

10 9 8 7 6 5 4 3 2 1

Also Available from Eye On Education

Common Core Literacy Lesson Plans:
Ready-to-Use Resources, K–5
Ed. Lauren Davis

Common Core Literacy Lesson Plans:
Ready-to-Use Resources, 6–8
Ed. Lauren Davis

Big Skills for the Common Core:
Literacy Strategies for the 6–12 Classroom
Amy Benjamin with Michael Hugelmeyer

Vocabulary Strategies That Work:
Do This—Not That!
Lori G. Wilfong

Vocabulary at the Core:
Teaching the Common Core Standards
Amy Benjamin and John T. Crow

Teaching Critical Thinking:
Using Seminars for 21st Century Literacy
Terry Roberts and Laura Billings

Rigor Is Not a Four-Letter Word, Second Edition
Barbara R. Blackburn

Math in Plain English:
Literacy Strategies for the Mathematics Classroom
Amy Benjamin

But I'm Not a Reading Teacher:
Strategies for Literacy Instruction in the Content Areas
Amy Benjamin

Teaching Grammar:
What Really Works
Amy Benjamin and Joan Berger

Active Literacy Across the Curriculum
Heidi Hayes Jacobs

About the Editor

Lauren Davis, Senior Editor at Eye On Education, develops and edits books for teachers and school leaders on literacy and the Common Core State Standards. Lauren is a regular contributor to Eye On Education's blog and is the author of a bimonthly column called "Comments on the Common Core State Standards." She also presents on that topic. Recently, she was one of three judges for Education World's Community Lesson Plan Contest.

Prior to working for Eye On Education, Lauren served as senior editor of Weekly Reader's *Current Events*, a classroom news magazine for students in grades 6–12. She also spent five years as Director of Language Arts at Amsco School Publications, a publisher of workbooks and other resources for secondary students.

Lauren has a master's degree in English education from New York University. She began her career in the classroom, teaching 7th and 11th grade English in New York City. She also taught 6th grade English language arts in Westchester, New York. She is passionate about engaging students in learning.

Special Thanks

The editor would like to thank Lesli Favor for her significant contributions to this book. Lesli is a former English professor who now writes full-time for publishers of books for school classrooms and libraries. She is the author of 59 English/language arts texts, nonfiction books, and leveled readers.

Contents

Note to Teachers xi
How to Use This Book xi

Part 1: Reading

Overview 1
Planning Checklist 1
Strategies for Helping Struggling Readers 2
Lesson Plans at a Glance 4

Lesson Plan 1: One Word at a Time: Doing a Close Textual Analysis .5

Lesson Plan 2: Meanwhile, Back at the Ranch: Parallel Plots and Story Pacing 9

Lesson Plan 3: Foreign yet Familiar: Images of Culture in World Literature 17

Lesson Plan 4: Are You Convinced? Analyzing a Speaker's Rhetoric 21

Lesson Plan 5: Where's the Logic? Analyzing an Argument 25

Lesson Plan 6: What's the Spin?
How Different Mediums Portray Things Differently 30

Lesson Plan 7: Time to Dig Deeper: Answering Text-Based Questions 33

Lesson Plan 8: This Is Not a Cardboard Cutout: Analyzing Complex Characters 39

Lesson Plan 9: Is This Satire or Serious?
Determining an Author's Real Point of View 44

Lesson Plan 10: You Had to Be There: The Impact of Setting 48

Lesson Plan 11: A Director's Liberties?
Comparing Film and Print Versions of a Text 53

Lesson Plan 12: Playing with Meaning:
How an Author Defines and Refines Words 56

Lesson Plan 13: What's This All About? Tracing Central Ideas 59

Lesson Plan 14: Is This Structure Sound?
Analyzing the Development of an Argument 62

Part 2: Writing

Overview 65

Planning Checklist 65

Strategies for Teaching Argument 66

Lesson Plans at a Glance 67

Lesson Plan 15: Strengthen Your Argument!
Developing and Distinguishing Your Claims 68

Lesson Plan 16: Where Do I Begin? Creating a Focused Research Question 72

Lesson Plan 17: Don't Just Google:
Using Advanced Search Terms to Find Information. 79

Lesson Plan 18: Quote or Paraphrase? How to Incorporate Sources 83

Lesson Plan 19: Collaborate in the Cloud: Contributing to a Class Wiki 87

Lesson Plan 20: Who's Reading This, Anyway?
Describing Information for Different Audiences. 90

Lesson Plan 21: What Comes Next? Using Colons Effectively 93

Lesson Plan 22: Reflections of a Writer:
Using Textual Evidence to Support Written Reflection .96

Part 3: Speaking and Listening

Overview 101

Planning Checklist 101

Strategies for Teaching Speaking and Listening Skills 102

Lesson Plans at a Glance 103

Lesson Plan 23: You're in Charge! Leading a Group Discussion 104

Lesson Plan 24: 'Dear Sir' or 'What's Up?' Language Depends on Audience 107

Lesson Plan 25: Teach, Don't Bore! Creating Engaging Presentations 112

Lesson Plan 26: Take Command of Your Audience! Presenting Your Findings 117

Lesson Plan 27: Sources, Sources Everywhere:
Integrating Multiple Sources of Information. 122

Lesson Plan 28: Good Evening, My Fellow Citizens: Evaluating a Speaker 127

Part 4: Language

Overview 135

Planning Checklist 135

Strategies for Teaching Vocabulary 136

Lesson Plans at a Glance 137

Lesson Plan 29: Are They Really Synonyms?
Understanding Shades of Meaning in Words 138

Lesson Plan 30: Get Your Ducks in a Row: Creating Parallel Structure 140

Lesson Plan 31: Everything in Its Place: MLA Style 146

Lesson Plan 32: If You Don't Get This Lesson,
   Explain It to Me: Understanding Paradox 150

Lesson Plan 33: Are Those Words Working Together? Using Hyphens Correctly 153

Lesson Plan 34: Know When to Break the Rules:
   Issues of Complex or Contested Usage 156

Lesson Plan 35: Notice Me! Notice Me! Vary Syntax for Effect 161

Appendix A: Selecting Rich, Complex Texts for Student Reading 167
Appendix B: Sample Argument Writing Prompts 171
Appendix C: Blank Lesson Plan Template 181
References 187

Handouts

Reading
   Identifying Logical Fallacies 28
   How Does the Media Spin a Story? 32
   Answering a Text-Based Question Step-by-Step 38
   How a Character Helps Develop a Theme. 43
   Compare Two Distinctive Settings from American Plays 52

Writing
   Research Activity Sheet. 77
   Which Search Engine Is Best? 82
   Ways to Incorporate Sources. 86
   Reflections of a Writer: Writing a Reflective Essay 99

Speaking and Listening
   Know Your Audience 110
   PowerPoint/Prezi Activity Sheet. 116
   Presentation Activity Sheet. 121
   Different Forms of Media 125
   Evaluate a Speaker and His or Her Speech 132

Language
   Identify Parallel Structure. 144
   Decipher Complex Conventions of Grammar Usage .160
   Analyze Syntax in Complex Texts. 165

Appendix B
   Checklist for Writing an Argument, Grades 9–10 175
   Checklist for Writing an Argument, Grades 11–12 179

Free Downloads

The handouts in this book are also available on Eye On Education's website as Adobe Acrobat files. Permission has been granted to purchasers of this book to download and print these handouts for free.

You can access the downloads by visiting Eye On Education's website: www.eyeoneducation .com. From the homepage, locate this book's product page by searching for the book title. Then click the link called "Log in to Access Supplemental Downloads" near the top of the page.

Your book-buyer access code is **CCL-7225-3**.

Index of Free Downloads

Identifying Logical Fallacies. 28
How Does the Media Spin a Story? 32
Answering a Text-Based Question Step-by-Step 38
How a Character Helps Develop a Theme 43
Compare Two Distinctive Settings from American Plays 52
Research Activity Sheet 77
Which Search Engine Is Best? 82
Ways to Incorporate Sources 86
Reflections of a Writer: Writing a Reflective Essay 99
Know Your Audience 110
PowerPoint/Prezi Activity Sheet 116
Presentation Activity Sheet 121
Different Forms of Media. 125
Evaluate a Speaker and His or Her Speech. 132
Identify Parallel Structure 144
Decipher Complex Conventions of Grammar Usage 160
Analyze Syntax in Complex Texts 165
Blank Lesson Plan Template. 181

Note to Teachers

As your school switches over to the Common Core State Standards, you are likely wondering how your classroom will look different and how your lessons will change. Eye On Education is here to help. *Common Core Literacy Lesson Plans* provides a variety of engaging and easy-to-implement lesson plans based on the standards. You can teach these lessons as they appear, or you can modify them to fit your particular needs. The book also provides ideas for revamping your current lessons to make sure they meet the standards and for creating new lessons to meet additional standards.

These lesson plans emphasize rigorous texts, questions, and tasks, which are at the heart of the Common Core. They also stress authenticity and metacognition. Students need authentic assignments that reflect the kind of work they'll be asked to do beyond school doors. They also need to understand how they are learning so they can eventually do it on their own. Authenticity and metacognition increase engagement. When students become aware of their learning processes and see the value in what they're being assigned, they take more ownership in what they are doing and are more motivated to work hard.

How to Use This Book

This book is intended for grades 9 through 12 English teachers, literacy coaches, and curriculum leaders. The lessons can be used in English and across the content areas. Interdisciplinary connections are included for many of the lessons because the standards emphasize the importance of literacy across the curriculum.

The lesson plans include reproducible handouts and links for further resources, and they can be extended from single lessons into full units (we provide ideas on how to do this). You can use each lesson as is, and you will learn how to create your own lessons based on these ideas. In that way, you will get a lot out of this book even when you are done teaching the lesson plans.

The book is organized by the strands of the Common Core State Standards—reading, writing, speaking and listening, and language. However, that sorting system indicates only the *main* emphasis for each lesson. In reality, each lesson incorporates more than one area. Reading, writing, speaking and listening, and language are integrated skills in the real world; they should be taught that way too.

Lesson plans are in order according to grade and skill level. Each lesson plan includes the following information:

- **Grade Level**—the main grade or grades for which the lesson is appropriate

- **Time Frame**—approximate number of class periods to complete the lesson. If you use extension ideas, time frames may be longer.

- **Overview**—general information about the goal and focus of the lesson and how to adapt it to other grades if applicable

- **Common Core State Standards**—Most of the lessons cover more than one standard because the standards are not meant to be taught in isolation. Note that we listed the standards the main lesson covers, but if you choose to extend the lesson based on the suggestions provided, you will incorporate even more standards.

- **Objectives**—what students will learn

- **Background Knowledge Required**—what students need to know before delving into the lesson

- **Materials Needed**—texts and other materials to have on hand for the lesson

- **Agenda**—detailed, step-by-step instructions for the lesson

- **Differentiation**—ideas to adapt the lesson for struggling and advanced learners

- **Assessment**—assessment ideas, including rubrics and scoring guides

- **Notes**—a place for you to reflect on what worked with the lesson and what you would change the next time

Reading

Part 1

Overview

To teach the Common Core State Standards in reading, you don't have to toss all your wonderful literature lessons and start from scratch. But you do need to look at your lessons and see if they match the rigor level the standards now require. If they don't, see what you can do to make them more challenging. Begin by making sure that your texts are complex enough and that they span the different genres the CCSS require. If they don't, see what you can swap out. Then look at how you teach the readings. The Common Core requires that students spend a great deal of time on the language of the text and that they respond to higher-level, text-based questions and tasks. If you teach *Romeo and Juliet* by having students make personal connections to the theme of love, that's fine but move that toward the end of your unit. Don't spend too much time at the beginning on the very general questions. Start with a closer look at Shakespeare's language, and make sure that students refer to the text when they answer questions and make inferences. For more tips to keep in mind when revising your lessons or creating new lessons, read the following checklist.

Planning Checklist

When planning a CCSS-based reading lesson, remember these tips:

☐ Choose more complex texts. According to page 4 of the Common Core State Standards Appendix A, you should consider these three areas when choosing complex texts:

- Qualitative measures—your professional judgment about a text's quality. Does the text have levels of meaning, such as satire? What's the purpose of the text, and what background knowledge is required?
- Quantitative measures—a more technical way to rate a text. You can use a scale such as a Lexile, which looks at word frequency and sentence length.
- Reader to text/task—your judgment as a teacher who knows your students! For example, is the text developmentally appropriate for your students?

Make sure to consider all three areas; don't rely on Lexiles alone. Lexiles can be misleading. For example, Hemingway's *The Sun Also Rises* has a grade 2 Lexile level because the language is relatively simple. However, you would never teach it in that grade. Use your professional judgment when choosing complex texts.

☐ Measure students' reading levels and monitor their progress throughout the year. You can use running records such as the Developmental Reading Assessment, Qualitative Reading Inventory, or Fountas and Pinnell Benchmark Assessment System. Or you can do your own fluency check by having students read something at the high end of the Common Core recommendations and then check for accuracy, fluency, and comprehension. Make a plan in your mind for how you'd like students to progress, and monitor them throughout the year (Calkins, Ehrenworth, & Lehman, 2012, p. 43).

☐ Teach short, challenging texts that can be read and reread so that students have plenty of opportunities to ponder meaning. Also teach extended readings so that students learn "stamina and persistence" while reading (Coleman and Pimentel, 2012, p. 4).

☐ If you haven't been doing so already, make sure to include literary nonfiction in your curriculum. Literary nonfiction, according to the Common Core, means stories built on arguments and with informational text structures, not stories and memoirs.

☐ Teach texts from a variety of "genres, cultures, and centuries" (Common Core State Standards, 2010, p. 35).

☐ Ask text-dependent tasks and questions. Help students learn to make valid inferences with text support.

☐ Provide opportunities for students to compare and synthesize multiple sources.

☐ Analyze informational and argumentative aspects of a story, not just its literary features (such as plot, setting, character, etc.).

☐ Create questions that build in a logical sequence. Don't start too broadly (as can happen with some kinds of prereading questions); pose questions that focus on the details of a text. After that, you can go broader and ask for students' opinions and personal connections.

☐ Some students will need scaffolding to understand complex texts. Scaffolding should not consist of "translating" a story or providing a brief synopsis for students to read ahead of time. Instead, scaffolding should help students with words and phrases so that they can determine meaning on their own. Here are some additional strategies for helping struggling readers.

Strategies for Helping Struggling Readers

- Model thinking aloud. For example, say, "I'm not sure I understand this word, but the author is writing about tornadoes, and the sentence right after uses the word *strength*, so I'm paying attention to how powerful tornadoes are."

- Focus on syntax. Students might need practice linking the subject to the verb. In complex texts, such as Shakespeare, the predicate often precedes the subject, which can be confusing for students. They might need to mark up the subject and verb until they learn how to read that kind of language more readily.

- Have students annotate the text as they read.

- Have students read some short texts (or small chunks of a text at a time) and reread them several times to ponder meaning. They can also listen to an audio version or read a text aloud to gain additional meaning.

- Teach when (and how) to use context clues and when to use reference sources to check word meanings.

- Use text sets. For example, if you're teaching Nathaniel Hawthorne's *The Scarlet Letter*, you may wish to pair it with articles about Puritanism in Massachusetts.

- Allow time for recreational reading, not just methodical close readings. Students need to learn to read for different purposes, including for entertainment.

- Create prereading activities as long as they do not spoil or give away the meaning and ideas of the text. Prereading activities might include help with vocabulary or with background information.

Lesson Plans at a Glance

Lesson Plan 1   One Word at a Time: Doing a Close Textual Analysis

Lesson Plan 2   Meanwhile, Back at the Ranch: Parallel Plots and Story Pacing

Lesson Plan 3   Foreign yet Familiar: Images of Culture in World Literature

Lesson Plan 4   Are You Convinced? Analyzing a Speaker's Rhetoric

Lesson Plan 5   Where's the Logic? Analyzing an Argument
        Handout—Identifying Logical Fallacies

Lesson Plan 6   What's the Spin? How Different Mediums Portray Things Differently
        Handout—How Does the Media Spin a Story?

Lesson Plan 7   Time to Dig Deeper: Answering Text-Based Questions
        Handout—Answering a Text-Based Question Step-by-Step

Lesson Plan 8   This Is Not a Cardboard Cutout: Analyzing Complex Characters
        Handout—How a Character Helps Develop a Theme

Lesson Plan 9   Is This Satire or Serious? Determining an Author's Real Point of View

Lesson Plan 10   You Had to Be There: The Impact of Setting
        Handout—Compare Two Distinctive Settings from American Plays

Lesson Plan 11   A Director's Liberties? Comparing Film and Print Versions of a Text

Lesson Plan 12   Playing with Meaning: How an Author Defines and Refines Words

Lesson Plan 13   What's This All About? Tracing Central Ideas

Lesson Plan 14   Is This Structure Sound?
        Analyzing the Development of an Argument

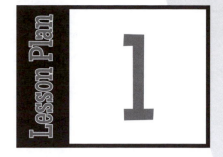

One Word at a Time

Doing a Close Textual Analysis

Grade Levels: 9–10

Time Frame: Approximately one class period

Overview: This lesson uses a well-known soliloquy from *Macbeth* as the text, but you can modify this lesson to work for a different excerpt from Shakespeare or from another playwright. This particular soliloquy was chosen because it is rich, is challenging, and requires reading and rereading to truly gain meaning from it. The CCSS emphasize the importance of reading and rereading passages to uncover ideas.

Common Core State Standards

- 9–10: Reading, Literature, Standard 4: Determine the meanings of words and phrases as they are used in the text, including figurative and connotative meanings; analyze the cumulative impact of specific word choices on meaning and tone (e.g., how the language evokes a sense of time and place; how it sets a formal or informal tone).

- 9–10: Reading, Literature, Standard 3: Analyze how complex characters (e.g., those with multiple conflicting motivations) develop over the course of a text, interact with other characters, and advance the plot or develop the theme.

- 9–10: Speaking and Listening, Standard 1: Initiate and participate effectively in a range of collaborative discussions . . . with diverse partners on *grades 9–10 topics, texts, and issues*, building on others' ideas and expressing their own clearly and persuasively.

Objectives

- Students will comprehend a short, challenging text.

- Students will analyze an author's choice of words and literary devices. Students will consider how those choices affect tone.

- Students will listen to an audio version of the passage and compare the speaker's tone with their own understanding of the tone.

- Students will look at the soliloquy in the larger context of the play, considering what the soliloquy says about how Macbeth has changed at this point.

Background Knowledge Required

Students should be reading *Macbeth* and should be in act 5, scene 5. Students should have familiarity with tone and connotation. They should also be familiar with literary devices such as repetition, alliteration, and metaphor.

Materials Needed

- Copies of *Macbeth* for each group (preferably not a version that includes a "translation" in the margin) or photocopies of Macbeth's final soliloquy (act 5, scene 5) if students are not allowed to write in their texts; pens and pencils for annotating the text

- A recording of the soliloquy (see Additional Resources)

Agenda

1. **Introduction**: Ask students to respond to the following with a quick show of hands: "Have you ever gotten a text or an e-mail from a friend and analyzed what the person wrote? You might have wondered about the tone—maybe it was hard to tell if your friend was mad at you or not. You might have wondered why your friend used a certain word to describe his or her feelings. Maybe you got a message from your crush, and couldn't figure out if he or she likes you back. Raise your hand if you've experienced this before. [Students raise their hands.] Okay, so that means you already have experience analyzing someone's words and feelings. You already have the skills to be good at today's lesson! Today, we are going to pay close attention to the words and tone in Macbeth's final soliloquy in the play and see if we can understand what he's really feeling and trying to communicate."

2. **Group Activity**: Organize students into groups of three or four. Give each group a photocopy of the soliloquy to mark up (unless students are allowed to write in their own books). Students should work together to translate each line of the soliloquy into their own words. They should circle words they don't understand (or that are used in a unique way) and make notes in the margins about what those words might mean. For example, they should try to determine what "petty" might mean in that context. They should use context clues and a reference source if necessary.

3. **Full-Class Discussion**: Have each group present its translations to the class.

4. **Group Activity**: Ask students to go back to their groups. This time, they should mark the literary devices in the soliloquy. They should label repetition "R," alliteration "A," metaphor "M," and so on. Students should discuss how those devices affect the tone of the soliloquy. For example, why would Macbeth repeat "tomorrow" three times? Students should also think about the connotations of Shakespeare's word choices and how those choices affect tone. For example, what is the connotation of "creeps in," and why might he have chosen that over a word like "enters"? Earlier, students figured out what Macbeth is saying, but what is his *tone* when saying those things? What is he really feeling at this moment?

5. **Full-Class Discussion**: Have students share their findings with the full class. What is Macbeth's tone in the soliloquy? How is his outlook on life different from what it was earlier in the play?

6. **Wrap-Up**: If time remains, play an audio version of the soliloquy for the class. What words does the actor emphasize? What is his pace? Does he interpret the tone in the same way that the students did? Ask students to jot down a few notes about how the audio version enhanced their understanding of the excerpt or was different from how they understood it.

Extend the Lesson

- Ask students to memorize the soliloquy. Explain why saying the words over and over in their minds helps them dig more deeply into the meaning and tone. It also helps them better appreciate the rhythm and the language. Sometimes a challenging excerpt has to marinate in your mind for a few days. Students can recite the soliloquy for you privately instead of in front of the whole class. Have students write brief paragraphs about what they gained from memorizing the soliloquy.

- Have students create a timeline of Macbeth's psychological deterioration. How does his outlook on power and on life change over the course of the text? Students should include at least five milestones on their timelines.

- Students can turn their timelines into full essays analyzing Macbeth's character. Students should be expected to use quotations from the text as evidence. You may need to teach or remind students how to incorporate quotations into their writing. For example, they need to introduce a quote and then summarize it; they can't just "throw it in." Have students consider when a quotation is necessary to prove a point and when it is not necessary.

- You may also wish to have students read excerpts from Machiavelli's *The Prince*, and compare it to *Macbeth*. How do the authors define power and how it affects a leader?

- You can have students read "Tomorrow and Tomorrow and Tomorrow," a short story by Kurt Vonnegut from *Welcome to the Monkey House*. Ask: "What is the theme of the story? Why did the author use a line from *Macbeth* as his title?"

Differentiation

For students who need extra support

- Have students study the soliloquy in smaller chunks and spend more time on each chunk.

For advanced students

- Students can find additional audio versions and compare them.

Assessment

- Look at students' annotated versions to see whether they looked at the text closely, word by word. Make sure all students participated in the assignment.

- If applicable, review students' notes about how the audio version enhanced their understanding.

Additional Resources

- A concise glossary of literary terms is available at highered.mcgraw-hill.com/sites/0072405228/student_view0/poetic_glossary.html.

- Several recordings of the soliloquy are available on YouTube, such as this one by Patrick Stewart: www.youtube.com/watch?v=HZnaXDRwu84&feature=related.

Notes

After implementing the lesson, reflect on what worked and what you would change the next time.

_____

_____

_____

_____

Meanwhile, Back at the Ranch

Parallel Plots and Story Pacing

Grade Levels: 9–10; adaptable to grades 11–12 (see note in Overview)

Time Frame: At least four class periods

Overview: Over the course of four class periods, students read or listen to the four parts of a story, create timelines for parallel plots, examine the story's pacing, and analyze the effects of these literary techniques on themselves as readers. Full-class discussions include text-based questions that require students to analyze and reread portions of the text to construct meaning and draw conclusions. Although ambitious, this lesson proceeds in a step-by-step manner that you can speed up or slow down, depending on your needs and time constraints. Some parts of the lesson function equally well as homework assignments. The lesson is geared to grades 9–10 but can be adapted to teaching Reading standards 1, 3, and 5 in grades 11–12. To do so, focus more on how the literary techniques contribute to overall meaning and aesthetic impact. In grades 9–10, Standard 5 asks students to analyze how an author's structural choices create mystery, tension, or other effects, whereas in grades 11–12, Standard 5 focuses on how an author's structural choices contribute to overall meaning and aesthetic impact.

Common Core State Standards

- 9–10: Reading, Literature, Standard 5: Analyze how an author's choices concerning how to structure a text, order events within it (e.g., parallel plots), and manipulate time (e.g., pacing, flashbacks) create such effects as mystery, tension, or surprise.

- 9–10: Writing, Standard 9: Draw evidence from literary or informational texts to support analysis, reflection, and research.

- 9–10: Writing, Standard 10: Write routinely over extended time frames (time for research, reflection, and revision) and shorter time frames (a single sitting or a day or two) for a range of tasks, purposes, and audiences.

- 9–10: Speaking and Listening, Standard 1: Initiate and participate effectively in a range of collaborative discussions . . . with diverse partners on *grades 9-10 topics, texts, and issues*, building on others' ideas and expressing their own clearly and persuasively.

- 9–10: Language, Standard 6: Acquire and use accurately general academic and domain-specific words and phrases, sufficient for reading, writing, speaking, and listening at the college and career readiness level.

Objectives

- Students will examine the four-part structure of Stephen Crane's "The Bride Comes to Yellow Sky."

- Students will map the parallel plots in the story and draw conclusions about the author's purpose in creating parallel plots.

- Students will examine the pacing of events in the story and draw conclusions about the author's purpose in pacing the story in this way.

- Students will analyze their responses as readers to the parallel plots and pacing of the story.

Background Knowledge Required

Students should be familiar with the terms *character*, *plot*, and *timeline* from previous grades.

Materials Needed

- Copies of "The Bride Comes to Yellow Sky," by Stephen Crane, available as an e-text from the University of Virginia Library: etext.lib.virginia.edu/toc/modeng/public/CraBrid.html. You will pass out parts I, II, III, and IV on separate days.

- Four sheets of poster or chart paper

- Dictionaries to use in the fourth class period

Agenda

1. **Introduction**: Tell students that one literary element they will study in this lesson is the idea of parallel plots. Prompt students' thinking by asking such questions as "Can someone tell me what a plot is?" and "Who knows what the word *parallel* means? What does it mean when two things are parallel?" Guide students to construct a definition of parallel plots: "two or more plots that happen at the same time in a story."

   To make the idea of parallel plots concrete, ask students to create timelines of their mornings, from the time they woke up to the time they arrived in your class. To make the activity time efficient, ask them to include only the main five events or so. Next, ask a few volunteers to read their timelines aloud. Point out that everyone's timeline was happening simultaneously, or "at the same time." If they were part of a story, they would be parallel plots. All the plots converged, or "came together," when this class started.

2. **Independent Reading**: Pass out copies of part I of the story. Explain that it is part I of a four-part short story, and today the class will examine the timeline of just this part. Give students time to read. Fast readers may finish in eight to ten minutes; slower readers may need 15 minutes or more. Those who finish early should write paragraphs that explain their reaction to the plot so far. Ask students to consider these questions:

   - What might happen later in the story?
   - What questions about the characters or their destination might be answered?

- How do they feel about the plot so far—curious? suspenseful? amused? something else?

3. **Small-Group Activity**: Organize students into small groups. Make sure at least one person who wrote a response paragraph is in each group. Members of each group should work together to create a timeline of events in part I of the story. Wrap up this part of the lesson by having groups share their timelines while you create a master timeline on a poster or chart paper.

4. **Full-Class Discussion** (second class period): Begin by asking those who wrote response paragraphs in the last lesson to take them out. Have a couple of volunteers read theirs aloud, and then open the floor to everybody to share responses. Even those who didn't write paragraphs last time can recall their reactions and describe them orally. Meanwhile, display the timeline for part I, and help students draw connections between their reactions/predictions and the events on the timeline.

5. **Read Aloud**: Pass out copies of part II of the story, and ask students to follow along as you read aloud. Reading this part will take approximately five to seven minutes. In the third sentence, tell students that *drummer* means "traveling salesman" (memory cue: his job is to drum up business).

6. **Full-Class Discussion**: Ask students to help you create a timeline of events from this part of the story, writing their input on a new poster. Then display the timelines for parts I and II side by side. Explain that these two plots of the story are parallel. Some of the events are happening at the same time but in different locations.

   Introduce the literary technique of *pacing* by telling students that Crane paced his story by splitting it into parallel plots. He took that a step further by separating those plots into separate sections. Although some writers might interweave parallel plots, Crane created separate sections for parallel plots. He doled out information in each plot bit by bit—another application of pacing. By giving readers information slowly and by switching from one plot to another, Crane controlled how quickly or slowly readers would be able to put the pieces of the story together. By making readers wonder and guess and gradually put the pieces together, Crane created suspense, tension, and curiosity in readers. Pacing a story also makes it more interesting.

7. **Writing Activity**: Wrap up the lesson by having students write a paragraph or two to explain their responses to the plot of the story so far. Ask them to think about the following questions:

   - What predictions or speculations might they make about what happens next in the story?
   - How do the events make them feel as readers? Curious? Suspenseful? Anxious? Something else?
   - What about the plot creates or causes their responses and predictions?

   Encourage students to refer to specific actions, characters, and details in the story to explain their ideas.

8. **Full-Class Discussion** (third class period): Have students take out and skim the responses they wrote during the last class period. On the board, create two lists. Label them "Moods of Readers" and "Predictions/Speculations." Ask students to

use ideas from their written responses to help you fill in the lists with ideas such as "curiosity" and "suspense" (moods) and "Scratchy Wilson will try to shoot up the saloon" (prediction). Encourage students to link their own and others' ideas to specific details in the story.

9. **Read Aloud**: Pass out copies of part III of the story. Ask students to follow along as you read it aloud. This will take approximately five minutes.

10. **Full-Class Discussion**: As before, work with the class to create a timeline for part III of the story, making a master copy for display. Display the three timelines to show that part I of the story is one plotline, and parts II and III together make a parallel plot. Go on to ask and discuss questions that will help students examine the purposes and effects of using parallel plots. Here are a few example questions:

    - Which plot does Stephen Crane introduce first? From what you know of the story so far, why might he have introduced Jack Potter's plot first?
    - Why would Crane begin the story by telling readers about Jack and his wife and then switching to the plot about the people in the saloon? Why separate the two plotlines in different sections of the story? Why not move back and forth between both settings and plotlines in smaller chunks without making separate story sections?
    - Part III of the story is short, just nine paragraphs. Why, do you think, did Crane set it off as a separate section?
    - Think back to your reactions when you had read only part I of the story. At that point, what did you think the rest of the story would be about? What did you think was most important to Jack and his bride? How did your understanding of where the story was headed change when you read part II? How did your understanding of the story change again when you read part III?
    - There is only one part of the story left. Based on what has happened in the parallel plots so far, what do you predict will happen in the final part of the story?

11. **Independent Reading** (fourth class period): Display the timelines, set to show that part I of the story is one plot and that parts II and III occur in that order in a parallel plot. Pass out copies of part IV of the story, and ask students to read it independently. Fast readers may finish in about five minutes. Those who finish early should use a dictionary to look up words in this or other sections of the story that were unfamiliar (e.g., what does a *livid* face look like? What is a *whelp*?).

12. **Full-Class Discussion**: Get students' reactions to the conclusion of the story. Was the final sequence of events what they expected in general? What point in this section marks the climax, or highest point of tension, in the story? How about the last paragraph—did they expect that particular resolution? Why or why not? Ask students to think back to part I and how it showed Jack and his bride lost in their own private, blissful world. Ask: "How did Stephen Crane use that to set up the intensity of part IV? How else did Crane build tension and suspense into the story?"

13. **Wrap-Up**: As a class, create a timeline for part IV of the story. Ask students to look at the existing timeline (showing parts I, II, and III) and to decide how to integrate the timeline for part IV. Students should recognize that the two plotlines in the

existing timeline dovetail into the plotline of part IV. The readers' anticipation and predictions about events in the first three parts are resolved in part IV.

Extend the Lesson

- Have students write informative essays on Crane's use of parallel plots and/or pacing in "The Bride Comes to Yellow Sky" (grades 9–10, Writing Standard 2). Students should

  - Use their responses and notes from class to plan their essays.
  - Use their planning to produce formal or informal outlines of their essays.
  - Write rough drafts that include an introduction, a body, and a conclusion (grades 9–10, writing Standard 4).
  - Use events or details from the story to explain their ideas (grades 9–10, Writing Standard 9a).
  - Workshop their drafts with a peer or writing group (grades 9–10, Writing Standard 5).
  - Revise their drafts in response to peer feedback (grades 9–10, Writing Standard 5).
  - Publish their final drafts in print or digital format to submit to you (grades 9–10, Writing Standard 6).

Differentiation

For students who need extra support

- Before students read Stephen Crane's story, teach a mini-lesson using *Blueberries for Sal* (see additional resources) or another picture storybook that uses parallel plots.

- Pass out the entire text of the story a week before you plan to use it in class. Encourage students to read the story in advance, independently or with a tutor, homework buddy, or helpful family member.

- Ask struggling students to serve as scribes to create their groups' or the master timelines. By focusing on a task that removes the pressure of providing insightful responses, they can participate. At the same time, by writing down key information, they are able to see, literally, the key points separated from the onslaught of information. Similarly, when you review timelines, ask struggling students to step in as "teacher" by reading the poster. When you review key terms, ask struggling students to check their notes and read or form definitions for the class; if the definitions are faulty, use whatever words you can from what students say and then build on them to create correct versions.

For advanced students

- Ask for volunteers (or choose students) to contribute to an oral reading of the story on the read-aloud days.

- Utilize advanced students' understanding of key concepts to create student-friendly explanations for struggling students. For instance, during class discussions, when you sense that some students are struggling, ask volunteers to explain the concept (e.g., parallel plots, pacing) using a different example—say, a movie or a popular book.

Assessment

- Have students work in pairs (threes will also work) to create a shared-writing product. The assignment is to write a paragraph that explains the literary technique of parallel plots. What is it? Why do authors use it? In addition, they should illustrate the definition with brief timelines that make up a story. For events in the timeline, they can refer to the personal timelines they wrote in the introduction on day one of this lesson or use selected events from "The Bride Comes to Yellow Sky." (They shouldn't try to use all the events because that would make the timelines too bulky for this purpose.) You can use this rubric to evaluate students' work:

Score	Criteria
4	• The paragraph explains parallel plots and why authors use this technique. • The timelines clearly and accurately show at least two sequences of events that happen concurrently at least some of the time.
3	• The paragraph explains parallel plots and why authors use this technique, though the explanation may be skimpy, vague, or weak. • The timelines show at least two sequences of events that happen concurrently at least some of the time.
2	• The paragraph explains parallel plots **or** why authors use this technique **or** the paragraph includes erroneous information. • The timelines show at least two sequences of events. This visual aid may be excessively skimpy or confusing.
1	• The paragraph gives ideas about parallel plots and/or why authors use them, but information is inaccurate or illogical or so poorly written that the paragraph doesn't make sense. • Some events are listed, but they don't help clarify the idea of parallel plots.
0	• Information is inaccurate or so poorly written that it doesn't make sense.

- Use the following rubric to grade the essay outlined in the lesson extension activity.

Score 4.0	The essay
	• Explains Crane's use of parallel plots and/or pacing. • Uses details from the story to explain ideas. • Has an introduction, a body, and a conclusion. • Organizes ideas logically (e.g., definition and example or cause and effect). • Gives accurate information. • Does not have pervasive errors in grammar and mechanics. No major errors or omissions in the score 4.0 content.

Score 3.5	The student demonstrates success at the 3.0 level plus partial success at the 4.0 level.
Score 3.0	The essay • Explains Crane's use of parallel plots and/or pacing, although explanation may not be rich or complex. • Uses details from the story to explain a few ideas. • Has an introduction, a body, and a conclusion. • Gives mostly accurate information. • Has some glaring errors in grammar or mechanics. No major errors or omissions in the score 3.0 content.
Score 2.5	The student demonstrates success at the 2.0 level plus partial success at the 3.0 level.
Score 2.0	The essay • Explains Crane's use of parallel plots and/or pacing, although explanation may be vague or contain errors. • Uses a detail from the story to explain one idea. • Contains numerous errors or misleading details or examples. • Has errors in grammar or mechanics that interfere with the reading or understanding of the essay. No major errors or omissions in the score 2.0 content.
Score 1.5	The essay demonstrates partial success at score 2.0 and 3.0 contents.
Score 1.0	The essay achieves partial success at score 2.0 content but not score 3.0 content.
Score 0.0	The essay achieves none of the writing tasks.

Additional Resources

- Another short story with parallel plots is William Faulkner's "A Rose for Emily." In this example, the shifts in plots show shifts in time (present and past events).

- A children's picture storybook that has parallel plots is *Blueberries for Sal*, by Robert McCloskey. If you introduce the book with good humor, students are likely to accept learning from the children's book—"I know you're not little kids, but this book will give you a clear idea of what parallel plots are; then we can move on to something more sophisticated." Puffin Storytime has a 2010 edition that includes a CD of a professional reading of the book—something that may help capture students' attention.

- The novel *Holes*, by Louis Sachar, has parallel plots. You might select excerpts to use.

- A local youth librarian may be able to suggest current or popular fiction that uses parallel plots.

Notes

After implementing the lesson, reflect on what worked and what you would change the next time.

_____

_____

_____

_____

Foreign yet Familiar

Images of Culture in World Literature

Grade Levels: 9–10

Time Frame: Approximately two or three class periods

Overview: The primary focus of this lesson is on the analysis of a cultural experience in a work of literature from outside the United States. Secondary focuses include answering text-based questions and analyzing theme. You can tighten the focus (and shorten the class time) of this lesson by emphasizing the analysis of the themes of poverty and political corruption and omitting or just skimming the themes of life and death. You can adapt this lesson to grades 11–12 to teach multiple themes (Reading standard 3) and irony (Reading standard 6).

Common Core State Standards

- 9–10: Reading, Literature, Standard 1: Cite strong and thorough textual evidence to support analysis of what the text says explicitly as well as inferences drawn from the text.

- 9–10: Reading, Literature, Standard 2: Determine a theme or central idea of a text and analyze in detail its development over the course of the text, including how it emerges and how it is shaped and refined by specific details.

- 9–10: Reading, Literature, Standard 6: Analyze a particular point of view or cultural experience reflected in a work of literature from outside the United States, drawing on a wide reading of world literature.

- 9–10: Reading, Literature, Standard 9: Analyze how an author draws on and transforms source material in a specific work.

Objectives

- Students will analyze the cultural experience portrayed in an excerpt of Colombian literary fiction.

- Students will respond to text-based discussion questions, citing details from the excerpt to support their responses.

- Students will determine multiple themes in the excerpt, tracing the ways specific textual details introduce and refine the themes.

- Students will examine ways the author draws on source material by examining a literary allusion.

Background Knowledge Required

Students should be familiar with the literary element of theme. They should know what an idea map is.

Materials Needed

- Copies of excerpt from "Death Constant Beyond Love," by Gabriel García Márquez, included in *Collected Stories,* by Gabriel García Márquez. New York: Harper Perennial Modern Classics (1999). Use the first eight paragraphs of the story.

- Dictionaries that are available during independent-reading time

- Oversize sheets of paper (e.g., 11 by 17) for idea maps

Agenda

1. **Introduction**: Introduce Gabriel García Márquez as a Colombian writer of novels, short stories, screenplays, and news reports. One of his most well known works is the novel *One Hundred Years of Solitude.* Introduce "Death Constant Beyond Love" by telling students that Márquez published the story in 1970. In it, a senator on the campaign trail stops at a village called Rosal del Virrey (Spanish for "Rosebush of the Viceroy"). Though you may be tempted to give an overview of what happens or to plant ideas for thought, the Common Core approach urges teachers to have students simply dive into the text and work out meaning as they go (with your guidance). With that in mind, pass out copies of the excerpt.

2. **Read Aloud**: Ask students to follow along on their copies as you read the excerpt aloud. This reading takes around seven to nine minutes. After you finish reading, point out that, as with most works of literature, one reading is like dipping your toes into a swimming pool. Say, "To get the full experience, you have to dive in. How do you dive in? You carefully reread the work, going as slowly and thoughtfully as you please, soaking up the ideas, drawing conclusions, asking questions, checking a dictionary to clarify words, and skimming back and forth to connect ideas."

3. **Paragraph 1**: Ask students to read paragraph 1 independently, marking up their texts to note key details, unfamiliar words, and important ideas. You might allow three to five minutes, knowing that students will add to their ideas during discussion. Next, ask students a few questions designed to get them to "dive in" to the text, keeping in mind that the purpose of this lesson is to examine the Colombian culture the excerpt reveals. Some overarching themes are poverty, corruption, life, and death. Here are some suggested questions:

   - What kind of village is Rosal del Virrey? (You might remind students that the name translates as "Rosebush of the Viceroy," and a viceroy is a governor.)
   - What is ironic about the name of the village? (The village's namesake is a rosebush, but no roses actually grow there.)
   - What two themes are introduced in the first sentence?

4. **Read and Discuss**: Taking the paragraphs one by one, repeat the reading and discussion process that you did with paragraph one. Here are some suggested discussion questions. As you go along, feel free to link ideas back to previous paragraphs. Note that this part of the lesson may take more than one class period.

Paragraph 2

- Why has the senator come to this village?
- Explain these things: "carnival wagons," "rented Indians," "gust of fire," "light-colored soup." (His traveling campaign is a virtual carnival; he hires people to make the crowd look bigger; the temperature is extremely hot in contrast to the air-conditioning in his car; sweat.)
- How does this paragraph advance either or both of the themes? (Hint: See last sentence.)

Paragraph 3

- What details help to reveal aspects of daily life in Colombia? In this town? (A few ideas: fried goat, electric fan, hammock, desert, the rose brought from outside)
- How does this paragraph advance either or both of the themes?

Paragraph 4

- What does this paragraph reveal about the nature of a politician in Colombia? What details help you build this idea?
- Notice the literary allusion to Marcus Aurelius's *Meditations*. In the fourth book of *Meditations*, Aurelius wrote, "Death is such as generation [i.e., birth] is, a mystery of nature . . . although not a thing of which any man should be ashamed." Now go back and look at the last sentence of the previous paragraph three. How does the senator's response to his own impending death compare to Aurelius's statement about death? Do you think these attitudes (Aurelius's and the senator's) are alike or different from attitudes about death in your culture? Explain.

Paragraph 5

- What campaign promises does the senator make to the people of this village? What do these promises tell you about life in this village? In Colombia?

Paragraph 6

- How do the paper birds extend one or both of the themes?
- Why are campaign employees setting up fake trees and make-believe houses? How does this activity help you understand the senator's goals as a politician? How does the activity serve to highlight, not hide, what living in this village is like?

Paragraph 7

- Notice the word *farce* in the first sentence. Who sees the "circus" of the campaign as a farce? Why?
- What campaign promises does the senator make now? What essentials of life do these promises correspond to? (Water, food, beauty)

Paragraph 8

- Is the senator sincere or cynical about his campaign promises? How can you tell? How might his approach compare to that of politicians in your culture?

5. **Wrap-Up**: Distribute oversized paper. Have each student choose a pair of themes, either life and death or poverty and political corruption, and write the theme pair at the center of a piece of paper. Have students use ideas and details from the excerpt and the class discussion to create detailed idea maps.

Differentiation

For students who need extra support

- Help students identify relevant details in the text to use to answer particular discussion questions, as opposed to asking them to find the details on their own. Then help students use the details to answer the question.

- Before discussing each paragraph, pass out copies of the discussion questions for that paragraph so that students can read and reread the questions at will.

- Allow the option of completing the wrap-up activity with a partner; however, to avoid the likelihood that an advanced partner will do all the work, pair struggling students together so that they can truly help each other develop needed skills.

For advanced students

- Ask volunteers to read paragraphs aloud as you proceed through the lesson.

- When an advanced student provides a basic answer to a discussion question, prod that student to think more deeply and link the answer to ideas or details in previous paragraphs, make inferences, and/or make comparisons to his or her culture.

Assessment

- Evaluate students' idea maps, using them to see how well students followed the discussion, how skillful they are at identifying relevant details in the text, and how simple or complex their analysis skills are. If desired, you can assign a grade based on a 4-point scale: score 4 = sophisticated analysis; score 3: thorough analysis; score 2: basic analysis; score 1: simplistic analysis; score 0: inaccurate analysis.

Additional Resources

- To extend the discussion of the themes of life and death, use Dylan Thomas's poem "Do not go gentle into that good night," available at Poets.org: www.poets.org/ viewmedia.php/prmMID/15377, and/or an excerpt from Tolstoy's *The Death of Ivan Ilyich*.

Notes

After implementing the lesson, reflect on what worked and what you would change the next time.

_____

_____

_____

_____

Are You Convinced?

Analyzing a Speaker's Rhetoric

Grade Levels: 9–10

Time Frame: Approximately one class period

Overview: This lesson uses Patrick Henry's "Speech to the Second Virginia Convention" as the text. However, you can replace that text with another seminal U.S. document or speech. You may wish to coordinate with a social studies teacher to choose a text that ties into what students are learning about history. The CCSS require the teaching of "seminal U.S. documents of historical and literary significance."

Common Core State Standards

- 9–10: Reading, Informational Text, Standard 9: Analyze seminal U.S. documents of historical and literary significance . . . including how they address related themes and concepts.

- 9–10: Reading, Informational Text, Standard 6: Determine an author's point of view or purpose in a text and analyze how an author uses rhetoric to advance that point of view or purpose.

- 9–10: Language, Standard 4: Determine or clarify the meaning of unknown and multiple-meaning words and phrases based on *grades 9–10 reading and content*, choosing flexibly from a range of strategies.

- 9–10: Writing, Standard 10: Write routinely over extended time frames . . . and shorter time frames . . . for a range of tasks, purposes, and audiences.

Objectives

- Students will comprehend an informational text of historical and literary significance.

- Students will closely analyze the writer's rhetoric and its effect on the audience.

Background Knowledge Required

It would be helpful for students to have some background knowledge about the context of Henry's speech. You may wish to begin the lesson by sharing the date of Henry's speech and asking students what was going on in the country at that time.

Materials Needed

- Copies of the text of the Patrick Henry speech, available here: www.history.org/Almanack/life/politics/giveme.cfm

Agenda

1. **Introduction**: Ask students if they've ever heard a convincing speech by a politician on TV or by a classmate who was running for student government. Ask what stood out about the way that the speech was delivered. Take some answers from volunteers. Tell students that today, they will carefully examine the rhetorical strategies speakers use to emphasize their points. You may need to define *rhetorical*. Write it on the board, and spend some time discussing it.

2. **Model the Think Aloud**: Do a think-aloud to help students understand Patrick Henry's rhetoric. First, distribute copies of Henry's speech to students. Read the first paragraph aloud to students, modeling the think-aloud process. Here is an example:

   Teacher Reads: No man thinks more highly than I do of the patriotism, as well as abilities, of the very worthy gentlemen who have just addressed the House.

   Teacher Thinks Aloud: *He's starting off by complimenting his audience. I wonder if they're on the same side politically.*

   Teacher Reads: But different men often see the same subject in different lights; and, therefore, I hope it will not be thought disrespectful to those gentlemen if, entertaining as I do, opinions of a character very opposite to theirs, I shall speak forth my sentiments freely, and without reserve.

   Teacher Thinks Aloud: *Okay, so he is about to present an opposing viewpoint, and he was just complimenting them so they wouldn't be insulted by his differing opinions. Interesting technique to begin with flattery. I wonder why his language contains a lot of extremes: "more highly," "very worthy," "very opposite." He is trying to be polite about the fact that he disagrees; he doesn't start with "you're wrong!" but it's clear that he does think they are wrong. Or is he exaggerating or being sarcastic? I wonder what he means by "opinions of a character very opposite to theirs." It doesn't sound like a minor disagreement; it sounds like he disagrees on much bigger issues.*

3. **Independent Work**: Now have students go through the rest of the speech on their own or with partners, thinking aloud and making notes in the margins about Henry's rhetorical strategies and word choices. They should mark up the text with their thoughts and questions. Walk around and check in with each student.

4. **Full-Class Discussion**: Have students share their observations.

5. **Wrap-Up**: Have students write a few paragraphs discussing Henry's rhetoric and how it helps convey his message. Students may disagree if they don't think his style is convincing.

Extend the Lesson

- Have students summarize the speech. Make sure students understand the difference between a straightforward summary and a review that contains opinions.

- Teach *logos, ethos,* and *pathos*. This site explains the words well: courses.durhamtech .edu/perkins/aris.html. Go through the speech as a class, and ask students to identify examples of each.

- Have students write speeches that use logos, ethos, and pathos. Their topics should be research-based and include evidence.

- Have students conduct research on how Henry's speech fits into history and what the reaction was at the time so they more fully understand the context in which it was delivered.

- Have students listen to the speech and write about the differences between hearing it and reading it. Ask: "On the audio version, where is the emphasis? What is the tone?" You can also have students practice reciting the speech in groups. There are six paragraphs. Organize students into six groups, and have each group practice a paragraph to deliver. They can split up the sentences or all say the paragraph at the same time.

Differentiation

For students who need extra support

- Spend time helping students with the difficult vocabulary words in the selection. Help students break the speech into smaller chunks and spend more time on each chunk. Continue the teacher read aloud with student input before having students work independently.

For advanced students

- Students can delve more deeply into some of the language choices and identify literary techniques used.

Assessment

- Look at whether students thoughtfully analyzed the speech based on your modeling.

- Evaluate students' paragraphs about the speech for understanding of how style affects meaning.

Additional Resources

- A recording of Henry's speech is available here: www.history.org/Almanack/life/ politics/giveme.cfm.

- Other great speeches are available at the American Rhetoric Online Speech Bank: www.americanrhetoric.com/speechbankm-r.htm.

Notes

After implementing the lesson, reflect on what worked and what you would change the next time.

_____

_____

_____

_____

Where's the Logic?

Analyzing an Argument

Grade Levels: 9–10

Time Frame: Approximately one class period

Overview: This lesson has students understand and evaluate the arguments in an Op-Ed piece from the *New York Times*. You can choose a different text for this lesson, as long as you choose a text that has a good mix of claims and evidence. The arguments don't have to be completely logical; the point is for students to be able to distinguish solid reasoning from logical fallacies. The text can be on any topic, as long as it is research-based and argumentative, not persuasive. See CCSS Appendix A, page 24 for the differences between the two terms.

Common Core State Standards

- 9–10: Reading, Informational Text, Standard 8: Delineate and evaluate the argument and specific claims in a text, assessing whether the reasoning is valid and the evidence is relevant and sufficient; identify false statements and fallacious reasoning.

- 9–10: Speaking and Listening, Standard 1: Initiate and participate effectively in a range of collaborative discussions . . . with diverse partners on *grades 9–10 topics, texts, and issues*, building on others' ideas and expressing their own clearly and persuasively.

Objectives

- Students will closely analyze an argument for logic and evidence.

- Students will identify common logical fallacies and why they are misleading.

Background Knowledge Required

Students should have prior knowledge of what constitutes an argument versus a purely informational text. Point out that the genres often overlap; arguments incorporate information.

Materials Needed

- Copies of the handout: Identifying Logical Fallacies, p. 28

- Copies of the *New York Times* Op-Ed article "Is There a Right to Lie?" www.nytimes.com/2012/02/20/opinion/is-there-a-right-to-lie.html

Agenda

1. **Introduction**: Ask students: "Have you ever argued with peers or adults and thought that they were just saying the same thing over and over without giving you real reasons for their opinions? That means you have experience identifying faulty arguments. What would have made their arguments more convincing?" Write students' comments about what constitutes a solid argument on the board. Say, "Today, we're going to look at arguments in greater depth."

2. **Mini-Lesson**: Distribute the handout on page 28. Spend time on the term *logical fallacy*. Logical fallacies include slippery slope, hasty generalization, begging the claim, circular argument, either/or, ad hominem, ad populum, and red herring. Read the examples as a class and have students create their own examples to make sure that they understand each one.

3. **Partner Work**: Organize students into pairs and pass out copies of the article "Is There a Right to Lie?" Have students read closely for meaning. Then ask them to annotate their copies, marking and labeling any possible logical fallacies that they are able to find. Share as a full class.

4. **Wrap-Up**: Ask students to find another argumentative article on their own (give them source suggestions) and mark it up for homework. Is the evidence presented with any errors in logic? How are those errors misleading? If there are no errors, how is the evidence logical? Allow them more than one night so that they can spend time choosing a solid article.

Extend the Lesson

- Coordinate with a social studies teacher and tie this lesson into work that students are doing on the U.S. Constitution and the rights of U.S. citizens.

- Tie this lesson into a larger unit on political campaign coverage and propaganda. You can also relate this lesson to *Animal Farm*, which explores propaganda.

- Have students write their own research-based arguments. Sample writing topics can be found on page 171 of this book.

- Have students apply the logical fallacies and propaganda techniques to advertisements.

Differentiation

For students who need extra support
- Spend more time modeling the process for students. Focus on fewer logical fallacies at a time.

For advanced students

- Have students read other arguments on the same topic as the *New York Times* article. Ask students to compare and contrast the arguments for logic and effectiveness.

Assessment

- Evaluate students' work on the handout to make sure they are able to understand the different fallacies and how they are illogical.

- Check students' homework to make sure that they were able to apply what they learned about logical fallacies to an argumentative article.

Additional Resources

- The site www.fallacyfiles.org contains additional examples of logical fallacies in the world. Students can even contribute to the site.

Notes

After implementing the lesson, reflect on what worked and what you would change the next time.

_____

_____

_____

_____

Identifying Logical Fallacies

Read the ten common types of logical fallacies that follow. Create an example for each or find an example from an article or advertisement.

1. **Circular argument**: A person simply restates his or her argument rather than providing new evidence to support it.
   Example: Oatmeal is good for you because it's a very nutritious way to start your day.

   Your example:

2. **Hasty generalization**: A person makes an oversimplified generalization without considering all the factors involved.
   Example: I'm sure that all the cereal from General Mills is made with too much sugar!

   Your example:

3. **Slippery slope**: A person concludes that just because one thing happened, a bunch of other things will definitely happen too—think of a gang of events running down a slope.
   Example: If parents don't allow their children to eat junk food, then eventually companies will stop making it, and people won't be able to enjoy a nice treat once in a while.

   Your example:

4. **Begging the claim (also called begging the question)**: A person provides a reason for his or her claim that is basically just a restatement of the claim.
   Example: Junk food should be removed from school vending machines because it is junk.

   Your example:

5. **Either/or**: A person assumes that there are only two options, or sides, without considering all other possible choices.
   Example: Either officials ban soft drinks from school cafeterias, or everyone is going to have health problems.

   Your example:

6. **Red herring**: A person avoids the main issues by discussing other points.
   Example: Junk food is not good for kids, but why are people always making life difficult for them?

   Your example:

7. **Straw man**: A person attacks an opposing argument by oversimplifying it.
   Example: People who don't support the ban on soft drinks must want everyone to get diabetes.

   Your example:

8. **Post hoc ergo propter hoc**: This is a faulty conclusion that just because one thing happened, then that must explain something else that happened.
   Example: I stayed up late last night, and I failed my science test today. I probably failed because I didn't get enough sleep and my brain wasn't sharp.

   Your example:

9. **Ad hominem**: A person criticizes someone's personality or character rather than examining that person's reasons and ideas.
   Example: The student government president's plan to solve the problem of the long lines at lunch is dumb because he's really selfish and cares only about himself.

   Your example:

10. **Ad populum**: A person tries to appeal to readers by discussing a larger, general concept (love, peace, democracy) rather than the specific issue at hand.
    Example: If you care about people getting along at this school, then you should vote for Jessica Smith for student government president.

    Your example:

What's the Spin?

How Different Mediums Portray Things Differently

Lesson Plan 6

Grade Levels: 9–10

Time Frame: Approximately one or two class periods

Overview: In this lesson, students will look at how different mediums represent a subject differently. This lesson meets Informational Text Standard 7. To adapt this lesson to literary texts, have students compare a subject or key scene from a short story or novel to two different artistic mediums.

Common Core State Standards

- 9–10: Reading, Informational Text, Standard 7: Analyze various accounts of a subject told in different mediums (e.g., a person's life story in both print and multimedia), determining which details are emphasized in each account.

- 9–10: Speaking and Listening, Standard 1: Initiate and participate effectively in a range of collaborative discussions . . . with diverse partners *on grades 9–10 topics, texts, and issues*, building on others' ideas and expressing their own clearly and persuasively.

Objectives

- Students will compare and contrast how different forms of media depict someone.

- Students will analyze why some forms of media focus on certain details about a person's life and other forms of media focus on different details.

Background Knowledge Required

No particular knowledge is required for this lesson.

Materials Needed

- Copies of the handout: How Does the Media Spin a Story?, p. 32

- Internet access for each student

Agenda

1. **Introduction**: Ask students whether any of them have ever googled themselves. Tell students to imagine they are famous, and there are tons of different resources about them online. Ask: "How would each resource portray you differently?" Students can take a minute to jot down some ideas or discuss this with a partner.

2. **Independent Work**: Have students choose a well-known person to research, such as a past president, the current president, an athlete or entertainment celebrity, or a cultural icon such as Steve Jobs. Tell students that it is their job to discover how different forms of media portray this person in a different light. Have students do research about their person using the handout on page 32. (You may want to stop the lesson here and do steps 3 and 4 the next day.)

3. **Wrap-Up**: Have students share their findings with the full class.

4. **If Time Remains**: Extend the conversation by asking students to discuss whether the media has a social responsibility to represent people in a fair and accurate light. Can freedom of the press go too far?

Differentiation

For students who need extra support
- Give students sample sources for each form of media.

For advanced students
- Encourage students to use forms of media that are not on the work sheet.

Assessment

- Check students' work on the handout and their participation in the full-class discussion.

Additional Resources

- Many articles about whether media spinning on celebrities goes too far are available online, including this one: abcnews.go.com/Nightline/Entertainment/story?id= 528898&page=1.

Notes

After implementing the lesson, reflect on what worked and what you would change the next time.

_____

_____

_____

_____

How Does the Media Spin a Story?

Look up information on a celebrity of your choice. How does each media form portray the person differently? Complete the table.

Media form	What does this form of media focus on about the person or make you believe about the person?	What does this form of media omit about the person?
Fan sites and photo galleries, including fake Facebook pages and Twitter accounts		
Videos		
Official biographies from sites such as biography.com		
Biographies on the person's own website		
Real Facebook pages for the person or the person's real Twitter account		
Another media source _____		

Time to Dig Deeper

Answering Text-Based Questions

Grade Levels: 9–12

Time Frame: Approximately two class periods

Overview: The Common Core requires that students identify evidence in texts to answer questions about the text. This is a shift from past pedagogical practices of asking for opinions, general observations, and personal responses that can be expressed without combing through a text's words, sentences, and paragraphs. Text-based questions enable deep discussions that require students to grapple with the words and ideas on the page to create meaning from the text. This lesson focuses on asking and answering text-based questions. "A Quilt of a Country," by Anna Quindlen, is the focus text, but you can use some or all of any complex text (literary or informational) that students are reading. You may want to consult with a social studies teacher and use a text that students are reading in that class.

This lesson is appropriate for students in grades 9–10 or 11–12. In all four grades, students are expected to understand what the text says and what can be inferred; in the upper grades, students have the added challenge of figuring out "where the text leaves matters uncertain."

Common Core State Standards

- 9–10: Reading, Informational Text, Standard 1: Cite strong and thorough textual evidence to support analysis of what the text says explicitly as well as inferences drawn from the text.

- 11–12: Reading, Informational Text, Standard 1: Cite strong and thorough evidence to support analysis of what the text says explicitly as well as inferences drawn from the text, including determining where the text leaves matters uncertain.

Objectives

- Students will read an informational essay and answer text-based questions about it.

- Students will practice going back to the text to look at what the text says explicitly, to make inferences, and to figure out where the text leaves matters uncertain.

Background Knowledge Required

No particular background knowledge is required for this lesson.

Materials Needed

- Copies of the Anna Quindlen article "A Quilt of a Country," available online at www.thedailybeast.com/newsweek/2001/09/27/a-quilt-of-a-country.html

- Copies of the handout: Answering a Text-Based Question Step-by-Step, p. 38

Agenda

1. **Introduction**: Tell students that today they will read and discuss an essay that appeared in *Newsweek* magazine on September 26, 2001. Pass out copies of the essay, and write its title on the board. Ask students to briefly explain what a quilt is and what *a quilt of a country* might mean. Remind students to look at the date that the article was published. Pass out copies of the article.

2. **Independent Reading**: Ask students to read the article independently. Encourage them to use active reading strategies that they may know, such as writing notes in the margin and underlining unfamiliar words.

3. **Full-Class Reading**: Ask students to listen and follow along on their copies as you read part or all of the essay aloud. Speak clearly and carefully, allowing students to hear the pronunciation of unfamiliar words and to hear the rhythm and cadence of the piece.

4. **Full-Class Discussion**: Lead students through an analysis of the text by asking a series of text-based questions. Each question should cause students to return to the text to reread a word, sentence, or paragraph in order to gather the facts or reasons needed to construct an answer. Text-based questions may ask why the author used a certain turn of phrase, why the author began with or emphasized a certain point, how the author illustrated or defended a point, how word choices created a particular tone or mood, which details revealed or supported a theme, and so on. Here are some suggested questions:

   - In the first paragraph, how does Quindlen compare the qualities of the United States to those of a quilt? How does she weave the quilt imagery throughout the essay?
   - What does the author mean by *mongrel nation* in the second sentence? Why does she return to that phrase in the second-to-last sentence of the essay?
   - Why does the author say, "You know the answer" at the end of the third paragraph? How does that affect the tone of the piece and her relationship with readers?
   - What does the author mean when she says people were concerned that "the left side of the hyphen—African-American, Mexican-American, Irish-American—would overwhelm the right"?
   - What can you infer about the author's childhood and her parents' neighborhood?
   - What questions does the text raise but not answer?

5. **Wrap-Up**: Have students complete the handout, following guidelines of your choosing (e.g., independently or in small groups, in class or as homework). (This might take more than one class period.)

Extend the Lesson

- Don't worry if you don't have time to cover all the questions during class time. You can use the additional questions to extend the lesson to another day, to use in a homework assignment, or to use as essay-test questions.

- Ask students to write text-based questions of their own, either in small groups or independently. The text could be the first three paragraphs of the essay, or you could assign the next two paragraphs and ask that the questions be based on that section. Use students' questions to demonstrate that close reading of a text hinges on individual words, phrases, sentences, and ideas. If students stray from text-based questions, explain that forming a personal opinion or judgment or describing one's personal reaction to the text is not the same thing as digging into exactly what the author is saying. Tell students that normally, a person can't ad lib a response to a text-based question. Wrap up by having students answer one of the student-generated questions, either in writing or as oral responses.

Differentiation

For students who need extra support

- Spend more time helping students work out the meanings of unfamiliar words. Ask them to use various strategies, such as context clues, peer input, and reference sources. Use class time to allow small groups to tackle one paragraph from the excerpt, discussing and verifying the meaning of each key word. Then have the groups report back to the full class.

- As homework, students could write paragraphs answering one of the text-based questions discussed in class. This reinforces the message that close textual readings require multiple readings of the same passage. A reader's understanding of a text deepens over time.

For advanced students

- Ask for volunteers to read parts of the essay aloud during the full-class reading.

- As homework, students might write paragraphs answering a text-based question that you did not discuss in class. As with struggling students, the advanced students will receive the message that multiple readings are beneficial, but they also will be challenged to find new connections and meaning in the text.

Assessment

- Check students' work on the handout to make sure they responded fully to all five steps of the process. Provide additional tips and examples for steps that students struggle with.

- Use the following rubric to evaluate students' written or oral responses to a text-based question.

Score 4.0	The student • Uses multiple words, phrases, or sentences in the text to answer the question. • Logically links the evidence (above) to the text-based question. • Expresses a clear answer to the question using the evidence and logic in the previous bullets. No major errors or omissions in the score 4.0 content.
Score 3.5	The student demonstrates success at the 3.0 level plus partial success at the 4.0 level.
Score 3.0	The student • Uses at least one word, phrase, or sentence in the text in the response. • Logically links the evidence (above) to the text-based question. • Attempts to express an answer to the question. No major errors or omissions in the score 3.0 content.
Score 2.5	The student demonstrates success at the 2.0 level plus partial success at the 3.0 level.
Score 2.0	The student • Refers vaguely to ideas in the text to answer the question. • Links (however loosely) the evidence (above) to the text-based question. No major errors or omissions in the score 2.0 content.
Score 1.5	The student demonstrates partial success at the 2.0 level; responses may identify evidence in the text but the student may fail to use it to answer the question or may answer the question without using specific evidence from the text.
Score 1.0	With help, the student achieves partial success at score 2.0 and 3.0 contents; responses are simplistic and limited.
Score 0.5	With help, the student achieves partial success at score 2.0 content but not score 3.0 content.
Score 0.0	Even with help, the student has no success.

Additional Resources

- You can find a list of curriculum exemplars for asking and answering text-based questions at the Engage New York website. Click through to an exemplar at your grade level to see a lesson plan, including the text and suggested text-based questions: engageny.org/resource/curriculum-exemplars.

- This page has an 11-minute video in which David Coleman, a contributing author to the Common Core, participates in a discussion about the role of text-based questions in classroom practice: engageny.org/resource/common-core-in-ela-literacy-shift-4 -text-based-answers/.

Notes

After implementing the lesson, reflect on what worked and what you would change the next time.

_____

_____

_____

_____

Answering a Text-Based Question Step-by-Step

1. Write the question that you were asked to answer.

2. Underline key words in the question that will help you focus your response. For example, does the question ask *why*, ask you to *compare* two things, or include a quotation from the text?

3. Reread the text. As you do so, list words, phrases, sentences, and/or ideas in the text that can help you answer the question.

    ▪

    ▪

    ▪

    ▪

    ▪

4. Think about how the evidence you gathered in step 3 can help you answer the question. Which pieces of evidence are strongest? Which link most logically to the question? Place checkmarks by the strongest pieces of evidence.

5. Write your response to the question using the strongest pieces of evidence. Be sure to link each piece of evidence to the question; don't just quote words randomly. Does the evidence help explain a metaphor? Does it provide a reason that supports the author's key idea? Does it help show how the author created a certain effect, such as a tone toward the topic or a mood in the reader? Identify this connection clearly for your reader.

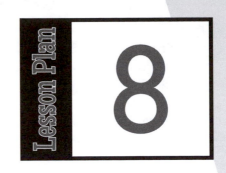

This Is Not a Cardboard Cutout

Analyzing Complex Characters

Lesson Plan 8

Grade Levels: 9–12

Time Frame: Approximately three class periods

Overview: Beginning with an in-class independent reading of an excerpt from a novel, this three-part lesson is driven by text-based discussion questions. The focus is on character analysis, and subtopics include plot structure and theme. Although this lesson uses an excerpt from Shirley Jackson's *We Have Always Lived in the Castle*, you can adapt or reuse this lesson with a work of fiction that students are already reading for your class or another work you choose.

Common Core State Standards

- 9–10: Reading, Literature, Standard 1: Cite strong and thorough textual evidence to support analysis of what the text says explicitly as well as inferences drawn from the text.

- 11–12: Reading, Literature, Standard 1: Cite strong and thorough textual evidence to support analysis of what the text says explicitly as well as inferences drawn from the text, including determining where the text leaves matters uncertain.

- 9–10: Reading, Literature, Standard 2: Determine a theme or central idea of a text and analyze in detail its development over the course of the text, including how it emerges and is shaped and refined by specific details; provide an objective summary of the text.

- 9–10: Reading, Literature, Standard 3: Analyze how complex characters (e.g., those with multiple or conflicting motivations) develop over the course of a text, interact with other characters, and advance the plot or develop the theme.

- 11–12: Reading, Literature, Standard 3: Analyze the impact of the author's choices regarding how to develop and relate elements of a story or drama (e.g., where a story is set, how the action is ordered, how the characters are introduced and developed).

- 9–12: Speaking and Listening, Standard 1: Initiate and participate effectively in a range of collaborative discussions . . . with diverse partners *on [grade-level] topics, texts, and issues*, building on others' ideas and expressing their own clearly and persuasively.

Objectives

- Students will analyze a character in an excerpt from a novel, tracing his motivations, decisions, and actions.

- Students will answer text-based questions to make connections between a character and the excerpt's sequence of events and between the character and the excerpt's theme.

Background Knowledge Required

Students should be familiar with the term *theme*, although this lesson reviews the concept.

Materials Needed

- Copies of an excerpt from chapter 8 of Shirley Jackson's *We Have Always Lived in the Castle* (New York: Penguin, 1962). Use pages 148–155, from the paragraph that begins "'Run,' Charles said at the front door, wrenching at the lock" (about halfway through the chapter) and going through the paragraph that reads, "'Constance,' I said, 'We have to run.'"

- Copies of the handout: How a Character Helps Develop a Theme, p. 43

Agenda

1. **Introduction**: Explain to students that they will read a short excerpt from Shirley Jackson's novel *We Have Always Lived in the Castle*. The excerpt begins just after Merricat starts a fire in the upstairs of the house, driven by anger and resentment toward Charles, a visiting cousin. The cast of characters in the excerpt, in order of appearance, is as follows.

    Charles—cousin to Merricat and Constance; he has come for a visit and is staying in the bedroom that had been Merricat and Constance's father's room when he was alive.
    Constance—Merricat's older sister.
    Merricat—the 18-year-old narrator of the novel; her full name is Mary Katherine Blackwood. She lives with Constance and Uncle Julian.
    Uncle Julian—uncle to Merricat and Constance
    Jim Donell—the fire chief
    Jonas—Merricat's cat
    Additional firefighters
    Villagers

2. **Independent Reading**: Pass out copies of the excerpt, and have students read it independently. Fast readers may finish in around seven minutes. Those who finish early should skim the excerpt again to strengthen their understanding of what happens and who does what.

3. **Character Analysis**: Use the following questions as the basis for either a full-class discussion or for small-group discussions, depending on the best fit for your class.

    - At what point does Jim Donell arrive?
    - When Jim arrives, what is his main objective for being there?
    - How does Jim's objective (from the previous bullet) contrast to Charles's? To Constance's? What details in the excerpt help you identify and contrast these characters' objectives?

4. **Analysis of Characters and Event Sequence** (second class period): Explain that the actions, decisions, and dialogue of characters drive the plot forward. Tell students to think of it as a chain of causes and effects: a character does or says something, causing an event or action to happen. As a result of that, a character does or says something, causing something else to happen. In any one scene (such as this excerpt), it is common for one particular character to drive the sequence of events, perhaps subtly. To examine the connections between characters and events in the excerpt, use the following questions to fuel a full-class discussion or small-group discussions.

   ▪ At first, how do the villagers respond to the fire?
   ▪ At what point does the mood shift, becoming darker? What lines of dialogue tip the mood toward menace?
   ▪ How does Jim first respond to the first signs of menace?
   ▪ What actions and dialogue serve to build the mood of menace?
   ▪ How does Jim's response to the menace in the crowd change? Why does it change?
   ▪ What action prompts the villagers to change from a menacing crowd to a destructive mob?

5. **Analysis of Characters and Theme** (third class period): Remind students that a work of literature's *theme* is its central idea or truth. Themes are sometimes expressed as phrases, such as "the loss of innocence" or "a fall from grace" or "a betrayal of friendship" and so on. Themes that lean toward being lessons or morals are often expressed in sentences, such as "Crime doesn't pay" or "You can't control destiny" or "Friendship comes in unexpected packages." How does an author build theme into a work? Within the work, the characters and events and dialogue work together to reveal the theme.

   Use the excerpt from Jackson's novel as an example. Tell students to think about the characters, actions, and dialogue in the excerpt and the ideas they generated through the discussion questions to discover the theme of the excerpt? Have students brainstorm as a full class or in small groups. Students should support suggested themes with specific details from the excerpt. Possible themes may include, but aren't limited to, "the downfall of a community," "a breakdown of leadership," "a lust for destruction," "the power of the individual," "hatred in action," or "Mobs will do what an individual alone would not do." These themes tie to details about Jim's actions and leadership as fire chief and the crowd's gradual loss of control.

6. **Wrap-Up**: Have students complete the handout independently.

Extend the Lesson
   ▪ Use any of the discussion questions or the handout itself as the springboard for a writing or speaking assignment.

Differentiation
For students who need extra support
   ▪ A week before this lesson begins, pass out copies of the excerpt for students to read in advance, either independently or with the help of a tutor, a friend, or an adult at home.

- Directly after the independent reading in class, have the class help you make a time-line of events on the board. This exercise will ensure that everyone has a basic understanding of what happened in the excerpt.

For advanced students

- Allow the option of completing the handout using a short work of literature that the student chooses, with your approval.

Assessment

- Pass out fresh copies of the handout, and ask students to complete it using a work of their choice, with your approval. You could provide a list of suggested works to help students make up their minds. Use the completed handouts to evaluate how well students are able to connect a character to the events of the plot and the theme.

- Use the following rubric to award points for students' participation and academic work during this lesson. A top score is 6.

Points to Earn	Task
1	Conscientiously reads or attempts to read the excerpt during the independent reading session.
1	Participates at least once during the discussion on day one.
1	Participates at least once during the discussion on day two.
1	Participates at least once during the discussion on day three.
2	Completes the handout with outstanding success.
1.5	Completes the handout with adequate success.
1	Completes the handout with limited success.
Top score: 6	

Additional Resources

In a search engine, type the words *character analysis hrw* to find a couple of model student essays, each one giving a character analysis. These are copyrighted by Holt, Rinehart and Winston—thus the *hrw* in the search term.

Notes

After implementing the lesson, reflect on what worked and what you would change the next time.

_____

_____

_____

_____

Name: _____   Date: _____

How a Character Helps Develop a Theme

Fill in each section of the graphic organizer using words, phrases, and/or sentences. Use details from the story to support your ideas when possible.

1. Title of work of literature:	2. Author:

3. First, you have this character whose name is _____

You think that this is the kind of person who

4. These are a few of the things this character does and says in the beginning:

-
-
-

5. These are some things that happen because of what the character does or says:

-
-
-

6. As all this happens, you start to notice that the character isn't exactly the person you thought he or she was. Now you see that the character is the kind of person who

7. When you think back over everything that happened, you see that a central idea helps you make sense of this character and the actions and events. This idea, or **theme**, is

Is This Satire or Serious?

Determining an Author's Real Point of View

Grade Levels: 11–12

Time Frame: Approximately one or two class periods

Overview: This lesson focuses on determining an author's point of view. In earlier grades, students looked at point of view by examining how an author develops characters or a narrator over the course of a text. In grades 11 and 12, students have to dig more deeply and uncover layers of meaning in a text in order to grasp point of view. Students must determine whether there is a difference between what is stated and what is really meant. This lesson gives students practice doing that through examining a satirical short story.

Common Core State Standards

- 11–12: Reading, Literature, Standard 6: Analyze a case in which grasping point of view requires distinguishing what is directly stated in a text from what is really meant (e.g., satire, sarcasm, irony, or understatement).

- 11–12: Writing, Standard 10: Write routinely over extended time frames (time for research, reflection, and revision) and shorter time frames (a single sitting or a day or two) for a range of tasks, purposes, and audiences.

Objectives

- Students will read a satirical story, looking at different levels of meaning and determining the author's real point of view.

- Students will practice doing their own satirical writing.

Background Knowledge Required

Students should be familiar with the term *point of view* from earlier grades.

Materials Needed

- Copies of the short story "A Modest Proposal," by Jonathan Swift. The story is in the public domain and is available online at a variety of sites, such as Project Gutenberg (www.gutenberg.org).

Agenda

1. **Introduction**: Tell students that they're going to read an author's unique proposal for how to solve a problem his community had. Pass out copies of "A Modest Proposal."

2. **Teaching Strategy**: First, read the full title and subtitle aloud to students: "A Modest Proposal for Preventing the Children of Poor People in Ireland from Being a Burden on Their Parents or Country and for Making Them Beneficial to the Publick," by Jonathan Swift, 1729. Ask students to make inferences—why might children have been seen as burdens for poor families?

    Now read the first two paragraphs aloud to students, or have student volunteers read them. In those first paragraphs ("It is a melancholy object. . . . " and "I think it is agreed. . . . "), the author describes the poverty in his country and reasons he thinks it's a problem that needs to be solved. Ask students if their inferences were correct and to decide what the author's point of view on poverty is so far.

3. **Independent Activity**: Have students read the rest of the story on their own, determining word meanings from context and writing comments in the margins. Tell students that their goal in reading is to determine the author's overall point of view on this topic.

4. **Full-Group Discussion**: Ask students to share their opinions about the author's point of view. "Is he serious about eating babies? Why or why not? How can you tell?" Teach students that this form of writing is called satire—a literary device that uses irony, derision, or wit to criticize a person or events. Review *irony* and *parody* if necessary and the ways they are different. Have students go back over the text and find evidence in the language that suggests parody. Here are some guiding questions you can provide.

    - How does Swift mock his topic or the people in his country? Provide specific evidence from the text.
    - What does Swift want readers to take away from this piece? Does he want to influence their beliefs on the topic?

5. **Independent Work** (to do at home or in class the next day): Tell students that it's time for them to write their own satires. Have them think of problems at school or in their communities and write brief satirical passages about the problems. You may want to review some satirical techniques, such as exaggeration and reversal, which are defined in this helpful guide: www.readwritethink.org/files/resources/lesson _images/lesson936/SatiricalTechniques.pdf. You may also wish to have students read more examples of satire (from the *Onion* and other contemporary satirical publications) before they do the writing assignment.

Differentiation

For students who need extra support
- Students may need to summarize each paragraph in the margins as they read to make sure they understand the text.

- Help students with difficult words whose meanings cannot be gleaned from context.

For advanced students
- Have students brainstorm for their satires by working in pairs; advanced students can be paired with struggling students to provide assistance.

Assessment
- Use the following rubric to assess students' satirical writing.

Rubric for Satire Writing

	4	3	2	1
Content	The student explains the topic thoroughly and uses satire throughout in an effective manner.	The student explains the topic and uses satire fairly consistently throughout.	The student makes some attempts at using satire but with limited success.	The student does not use satire effectively or accurately.
Organization	The writing has a clear organizational pattern and is easy to follow.	The writing has an organizational pattern that is mostly easy to follow.	The writing is organized in a confusing manner.	The writing lacks organization and is difficult to follow.
Language	The language is specific and vivid and brings the satire to life.	The language is clear though it may lack some luster or precision.	The language is a bit unclear at times or is not sharp or varied.	The language is unclear, imprecise, or confusing.
Conventions	There are few mistakes in grammar and/or conventions.	There are some mistakes in grammar and/or conventions, but they do not affect readability.	There are a good number of mistakes in grammar and/or conventions that affect readability.	Numerous errors are present in grammar and usage; these errors make readability a problem.

Additional Resources

- PBS has great ideas for teaching political analysis through satire: www.pbs.org/now/classroom/satire.html.

- The *New York Times* Learning Network has an engaging lesson plan that uses an article about the movie *Anchorman* to get students thinking about news satires: http://learning.blogs.nytimes.com/2004/07/19/fighting-fire-with-satire/

- Use the satirical newspaper the *Onion* to engage students in satire and have them write their own satirical pieces: www.theonion.com.

Notes

After implementing the lesson, reflect on what worked and what you would change the next time.

_____

_____

_____

_____

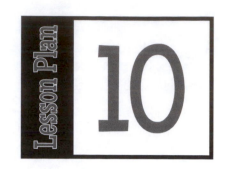

You Had to Be There

The Impact of Setting

Grade Levels: 11–12

Time Frame: Approximately two class periods

Overview: This lesson focuses tightly on setting as an element of literature. For texts, it uses the scene descriptions from two plays, one by Susan Glaspell and one by Eugene O'Neill. You can easily substitute scene descriptions from plays of your own choosing. Similarly, you could adapt this lesson to use one or two short stories of your choice.

Common Core State Standards

- 11–12: Reading, Literature, Standard 3: Analyze the impact of the author's choices regarding how to develop and relate elements of a story or drama (e.g., where a story is set, how the action is ordered, how the characters are introduced and developed).

- 11–12: Reading, Literature, Standard 9: Demonstrate knowledge of eighteenth-, nineteenth-, and early-twentieth-century foundational works of American literature, including how two or more texts from the same period treat similar themes or topics.

- 11–12: Speaking and Listening, Standard 1: Initiate and participate effectively in a range of collaborative discussions . . . with diverse partners on *grades 11–12 topics, texts, and issues*, building on others' ideas and expressing their own clearly and persuasively.

Objectives

- Students will analyze details of setting in two plays by American playwrights.

- Students will draw conclusions that connect details of setting to characterization and plot.

Background Knowledge Required

No particular background knowledge is required for this lesson.

Materials Needed

- Copies of the scene description from Susan Glaspell's *Trifles* through "other signs of incompleted work." The play is available as an e-text from the University of Virginia Library: etext/virginia.edu/toc/modeng/public/GlaTrif.html.

- Copies of the scene description from Eugene O'Neill's *Long Day's Journey into Night*, through "Sunshine comes through the windows at right." The play is available on Amazon or Google Books.

- Copies of the handout: Compare Two Distinctive Settings from American Plays, p. 52

Agenda

1. **Introduction**: Tell students that today they will look closely at a literary element that is often taken for granted yet can be of the utmost importance to a narrative. This element is setting. Tell students that you want them to play around with the idea of setting before you dive into the literary examples. On the board, write, "The Setting of ME!" Organize students into groups of two or three. Each student should describe a setting that best reflects who he or she is (e.g., a bedroom at home, a sports field, a place in nature). As a student describes a setting, the other group members should use details in the description to draw conclusions about the speaker. For example, "You love to play the flute" or "You have a phobia about dust bunnies." Once the speaker finishes his or her description, the listener(s) should respond by sharing and explaining their conclusions.

   Explain that just as a setting can reveal truths about a person who loves it or lives in it, so do settings in literature help reveal truths about characters and their actions. Remind students that setting includes not only the physical environment but also time in history, time of day, season of year, weather, and so on. A good way to study setting is to examine playwrights' descriptions of the settings of plays. These descriptions are often direct and detailed. In contrast, authors of stories and poems often weave details and hints about setting throughout the work instead of putting all the description up front.

2. **Read Aloud 1**: Pass out copies of the Glaspell excerpt. Ask students to follow along as you read it aloud. The reading should take around three minutes. Ask students to think about what they heard and try to form a mental image of the setting. Then ask them to listen as you read the excerpt again. This time, they should mark up their excerpts to draw attention to key details of the setting. When you finish reading, give students five more minutes to jot down conclusions that they can draw from details in the setting. For example, the hand pump in the kitchen sink suggests that the setting is a long time ago, when people didn't have piped-in water.

3. **Full-Class Discussion**: Engage students in a discussion in which they share their conclusions and the supporting details. As students share ideas, work in some questions to help them think about the impact of the setting. Here are a few examples:

   - What kinds of people might live in this setting? What kinds of people would not? (Think about occupation, level of wealth, and place in society, for example.)
   - What can you tell about the lives of the people who live here? (Think about daily activities, for example, and the fact that this is a room in a private home as opposed to a public place.)
   - What kinds of action might happen in this setting? How does this setting limit the types of events that might happen?

4. **Read Aloud 2** (second class period): Pass out copies of the O'Neill excerpt and repeat the process that you used for the Glaspell excerpt (agenda items 2 and 3). It takes around four or five minutes to read the O'Neill excerpt aloud.

5. **Wrap-Up**: Have students summarize what they learned in this lesson by completing the handout.

Extend the Lesson

- Have students read the complete text of *Trifles* and trace the impact of the details of the setting (which are some of the "trifles" of the play's title) on characterization, events, and dialogue. Students should connect the rustic and dreary kitchen to the characterization of Mrs. Wright as unhappy and beaten down by her marriage to John Wright. When the visiting men make fun of the state of Mrs. Wright's kitchen and draw disparaging conclusions about her, students should see the connection between the details of setting and characterization *and* plot. Within this setting, with this characterization, and with the props of the broken bird cage and dead bird in the pretty box, Mrs. Wright's murder of her husband makes sense. Her desperate surroundings reflect her desperation in life and her desperate act.

Differentiation

For students who need extra support

- If most of the class is likely to struggle with the inclusion of two excerpts, design your lesson around just *Trifles*, extending it to include a reading of the entire play (see the lesson extension idea). Spend more time showing the connections between details of the setting and characterization, dialogue, actions, and general plot development.

For advanced students

- Pass out a list of the discussion questions before beginning the discussion, and allow students time to read the questions and jot down an idea or two per question; this preparation benefits both struggling and advanced students. Then assign discussion questions to various advanced students, asking each to serve as discussion leader for her or his question.

Assessment

- Evaluate the handouts, assigning scores as follows: score 4: advanced; score 3: proficient; score 2: novice with some knowledge; score 1: beginner with little knowledge; score 0: non-participant.

Additional Resources

- Glaspell adapted *Trifles* into a short story, "A Jury of Her Peers."

- O'Neill's *Long Day's Journey into Night* was made into a movie by the same name.

Notes

After implementing the lesson, reflect on what worked and what you would change the next time.

_____

_____

_____

_____

Compare Two Distinctive Settings from American Plays

Use details from the setting of each play to fill in the graphic organizer. If the excerpt you read does not reveal a detail, write "n/a."

	Trifles, by Susan Glaspell	*Long Day's Journey into Night,* by Eugene O'Neill
Time in history		
Time of year		
Weather		
Type of house and room in house		
Physical details of room		
Mood of room (*Hint: use one or more adjectives that describe how the room makes you feel*)		

A Director's Liberties?

Comparing Print and Film Versions of a Text

Grade Levels: 11–12

Time Frame: Approximately four class periods

Overview: In this lesson, students will compare the text of *A Raisin in the Sun* to a film version. *A Raisin in the Sun* was chosen as the sample text because it's a rich text and because the Common Core requires one play by an American dramatist. If you wish, you can do this lesson with a different American play or with a Shakespearean play.

Common Core State Standards

- 11–12: Reading, Literature, Standard 7: Analyze multiple interpretations of a story, drama, or poem (e.g., recorded or live production of a play or recorded novel or poetry), evaluating how each version interprets the source text. (Include at least one play by Shakespeare and one play by an American dramatist.)

- 11–12: Speaking and Listening, Standard 1: Initiate and participate effectively in a range of collaborative discussions . . . with diverse partners on *grades 11–12 topics, texts, and issues*, building on others' ideas and expressing their own clearly and persuasively.

Objectives

- Students will view the film version of a play they have read in class and analyze and discuss the director's decisions to adhere to or stray from the text.

- Students will think critically about the benefits and drawbacks of reading a play versus viewing it.

Background Knowledge Required

Students should have completed reading the play at this point. If not, then you can just show the parts of the movie that correspond with what they have read thus far.

Materials Needed

- A DVD of one of the following three productions of *A Raisin in the Sun*: the 1961 version, starring Sidney Poitier; the 1989 version, starring Danny Glover; or the 2008 version, starring Sean (P. Diddy) Combs

- A copy of the play for each student, preferably one that students can mark up by hand or with electronic notes.

Agenda

1. **Introduction**: Tell students that today, you're not their teacher; you're a Hollywood director! You're directing a movie version of *A Raisin in the Sun*, and you have hired your students as production assistants.

2. **Group Work**: Organize students into five groups of three or four. Assign each group to one of the following areas: casting, lighting, costumes, sets, and music. Groups should make notes on how they envision their aspect of the movie. Require each group to use evidence from the text to support their decisions. For example, if the casting assistants would like to cast Viola Davis as Mama, they should have specific reasons based on how she's described in the text and what they know about the actress. When groups have made their selections, they should present their ideas to the full class.

   Note that you may want to give students vocabulary terms used in film and theater. You can provide five terms for each of the assigned groups. For example, the language of casting might be *stock characters, typecast, playing against type, stereotype, prototype, ensemble, principals, supporting cast.*

3. **Full-Class Activity** (next two or three days): Now have students watch the movie version and take notes on all the elements—casting, lighting, sets, costumes, and music.

4. **Wrap-Up**: Have students share what they thought of the director's decisions, including how they differ from their own interpretations. For homework, have students write brief essays discussing the benefits and drawbacks of reading versus viewing the play. The essays should particularly address what is gained and lost in each medium.

Extend the Lesson

- Have students read online reviews of the movie version of *A Raisin in the Sun* and write their own reviews of the film.

Differentiation

For students who need extra support

- Provide more examples of how to find evidence in the text for making decisions on lighting, music, sets, costumes, and casting.

For advanced students

- Students can evaluate the actors' performances and how they delivered the lines. Did their delivery change how the students interpreted the tone and meaning of the scenes?

Assessment

- Evaluate whether students used evidence from the text to support their decisions about lighting, music, sets, costumes, or casting.

- Check students' homework for evidence of critical thinking about the differences between text and film.

Additional Resources

- A review of the Broadway version is available here: www.ew.com/ew/article/0,,631552,00.html

- Here is another lesson plan for comparing text to film: www.readwritethink.org/classroom-resources/lesson-plans/reel-scoop-comparing-books-46.html.

Notes

After implementing the lesson, reflect on what worked and what you would change the next time.

_____

_____

_____

_____

Playing with Meaning

How an Author Defines and Refines Words

Grade Levels: 11–12; can be adapted to grades 9–10 (see note in Overview)

Time Frame: Approximately one class period

Overview: In this lesson, students take a close look at a key term used in a text. To adapt this lesson for students in grades 9–10, have students analyze how word choices affect a text's meaning and tone but don't require the extra step of examining how the author *refines* a word's meaning throughout the course of the text.

This lesson uses President Franklin Roosevelt's 1941 "Annual Message to Congress" or "Four Freedoms" speech. You may want to work with a social studies teacher and do this lesson when students are learning about that period in history.

Common Core State Standards

- 11–12: Reading, Informational Text, Standard 4: Determine the meanings of words and phrases as they are used in a text, including figurative, connotative, and technical meanings; analyze how an author uses and refines the meaning of a key term or terms over the course of a text (e.g., how Madison defines *faction* in Federalist No. 10).

- 9–10: Reading, Informational Text, Standard 4: Determine the meanings of words and phrases as they are used in a text, including figurative, connotative, and technical meanings; analyze the cumulative impact of specific word choices on meaning and tone (e.g., how the language of a court opinion differs from that of a newspaper).

- 9–12: Writing, Standard 10: Write routinely over extended time frames . . . and shorter time frames . . . for a range of tasks, purposes, and audiences.

Objectives

- Students will read an informational text and identify the key terms in the text.

- Students will analyze how an author uses and changes or maintains a word's meaning throughout the text.

Background Knowledge Required

Students should have experience looking closely at word meanings in a text.

Materials Needed

- Copies of FDR's "Four Freedoms" speech: www.ourdocuments.gov/doc.php?flash= true&doc=70&page=transcript

Agenda

1. **Introduction**: Ask students to work with partners to make a quick list of the qualities of effective speeches. Have each pair share with the full class.

2. **Reading Lesson**: Tell students that today, they are going to read a speech that is well known for its power and use of language. The speech is President Franklin Roosevelt's 1941 Message to Congress. Pass out copies of the speech. Read the first paragraph aloud to students, and ask them what "unprecedented" moment in history he might mean. Ask students to read the rest of the speech independently and circle words that they find particularly powerful or interesting.

3. **Class Discussion**: Have students say which big concept words they found interesting in the speech. Ask: "How do those words create a particular tone?" Then ask which words were repeated the most. Discuss the word *freedom*. Ask students if they can define *freedom* according to President Roosevelt. Does his definition change throughout the text? Students should use evidence from the text in their answers. You may wish to have them reread the last part of the speech, which focuses on the four freedoms, to answer this question or reread that part aloud along with students. Take notes on the board as students attempt to understand the president's different uses of the word *freedom*.

4. **Wrap-Up**: Have students write a few paragraphs about how FDR defined freedom and how that definition is similar to or different from their definitions of freedom today.

Differentiation

For students who need extra support

- Use an excerpt rather than the whole speech. Point out certain interesting words and phrases, and help students with challenging vocabulary.

For advanced students

- Have students who are skilled readers share their thoughts about repetition of the word *freedom* as well as other examples of repetition throughout the text and how that creates a rhythm and makes the speech more powerful.

Assessment

- Assess students' paragraphs about the speech, making sure they used evidence from the text to support their points. Make sure students tied the president's definition of *freedom* to their own definitions rather than jumping straight to their own thoughts and opinions.

Additional Resources

- A recording of the speech is available here: www.youtube.com/watch?v= QnrZUHcpoNA.

Notes

After implementing the lesson, reflect on what worked and what you would change the next time.

_____

_____

_____

_____

What's This All About?

Tracing Central Ideas

Grade Levels: 11–12; can be adapted to grades 9–10 (see note in Overview)

Time Frame: Approximately one class period, not including the time it takes for students to read the book

Overview: Standard 2 for Informational Texts has 11th and 12th graders determine two or more central ideas of a text and see how they develop. Students should not figure out central ideas just when they finish reading but should think about big ideas along the way so they can analyze the author's treatment of those ideas. This lesson uses Gladwell's *The Tipping Point* but can be done with any rich, complex informational text. To adapt this lesson down to grades 9 and 10, have students trace one idea, not two.

Common Core State Standards

- 11–12: Reading, Informational Text, Standard 2: Determine two or more central ideas of a text and analyze their development over the course of the text, including how they interact and build on each other to provide a complex analysis; provide an objective summary of the text.

- 9–10: Reading, Informational Text, Standard 2: Determine a central idea of a text and analyze its development over the course of the text, including how it emerges and is shaped and refined by specific details; provide an objective summary of the text.

- 9–12: Writing, Standard 4: Produce clear and coherent writing in which the development, organization, and style are appropriate to task, purpose, and audience.

Objectives

- Students will identify at least two central ideas in a text.

- Students will trace how the central ideas interact and build on each other throughout the text.

Background Knowledge Required

Students should have prior experience determining the main idea(s) of a text. Students should have begun reading *The Tipping Point* but should not be past the introduction. Students should also be familiar with summary writing.

Materials Needed

- Copies of *The Tipping Point*, by Malcolm Gladwell. If time is an issue, you can have students read an excerpt from the book rather than the whole book. This lesson is designed for the whole book but could also work with just chapter 2, "The Law of the Few."

Agenda

1. **Introduction**: Tell students that they're just starting to see what Gladwell might mean by a "tipping point." Ask: "Based on Gladwell's introduction, what are two central ideas he's going to explore in the text? How do you know?" (Possible answers: behavior is contagious; little causes can have big effects.) You can have students do this work with partners rather than with the full class.

2. **Independent Work**: Tell students their job going forward is to read as though they were detectives and trace how those ideas are developed throughout the book. Have students make three-column charts in their notebooks. One column should be for the first central idea, one column should be for the second central idea, and one column should be for ways the ideas come together. Tell students to make notes on this chart as they read the book. The notes should include specific evidence from the text (with page numbers) that supports each central idea.

3. **Writing Activity**: When students finish the book, have them write objective summaries of the text. The summaries should synthesize the two central ideas and explain how they come together (or where they diverge) to form Gladwell's idea of a tipping point. You may need to review with students the term *objective* and the difference between a summary and a review.

Differentiation

For students who need extra support

- Have students read smaller chunks of the text at a time, and help them with difficult words and sentences.

For advanced students

- Encourage students to discuss two or more central ideas if they would like.

Assessment

- Check students' notebooks to make sure they are taking notes from the text as they read.

- You may want to use the following scoring guide for summary writing.

Scoring Guide for Summaries

Category	Possible Points	Points Earned
The summary focuses on the central ideas and includes relevant facts and details.	5	
The summary is well organized and easy to follow.	5	
The summary is written in objective language without opinions or editorializing.	5	
The summary follows the conventions of standard English and contains minimal errors in grammar, usage, spelling, and punctuation.	5	
TOTAL	20	

Additional Resources

- This lesson includes good pointers for students to keep in mind when writing summaries: suite101.com/article/how-to-write-a-summary-a107532.

Notes

After implementing the lesson, reflect on what worked and what you would change the next time.

_____

_____

_____

_____

Is This Structure Sound?

Analyzing the Development of an Argument

Grade Levels: 11–12; can be adapted to grades 9–10 (see note in Overview)

Time Frame: Approximately two class periods

Overview: In this lesson, students analyze the structure of an informational text. This lesson is designed for 11th and 12th graders. To adapt the lesson down for 9th and 10th graders, have students look at how the structure of the text helps an author develop his or her ideas but don't include the added step of determining whether the structure makes the ideas convincing and engaging.

This lesson is based on Gladwell's *The Tipping Point* and was designed to be used with Lesson Plan 13; however, you can adapt this lesson to work with any informational text.

Common Core State Standards

- 11–12: Reading, Informational Text, Standard 5: Analyze and evaluate the effectiveness of the structure an author uses in his or her exposition or argument, including whether the structure makes points clear, convincing, and engaging.

- 9–10: Reading, Informational Text, Standard 5: Analyze in detail how an author's ideas or claims are developed and refined by particular sentences, paragraphs, or larger portions of a text (e.g., a section or chapter).

- 9–12: Speaking and Listening, Standard 1: Initiate and participate effectively in a range of collaborative discussions . . . with diverse partners *on [grade-level] topics, texts, and issues,* building on others' ideas and expressing their own clearly and persuasively.

Objectives

- Students will analyze an author's structure and how it helps that author convey a message.

- Students will analyze the effect a text structure has on readers.

Background Knowledge Required

Students should have some familiarity with basic text structures, such as problem-solution, cause-effect, and compare-contrast. This lesson should be done after students finish or are close to finishing a text (*The Tipping Point* or a text of your own choosing).

Materials Needed:

- Copies of Malcolm Gladwell's *The Tipping Point*

Agenda

1. **Introduction**: Tell students that *The Tipping Point* was on the *New York Times* best-seller list for a long time. Ask students what makes an informational book such as *The Tipping Point* interesting and easy to read. Compile their responses on the board. Students might say something about the way it is organized; if not, ask them a question about whether the organization is easy to follow. Tell students that a book can't just have good ideas; the author also has to explain those ideas in ways that are clear and interesting to others. Tell students they are going to do a little surgery and take apart Gladwell's structure to see whether it is solid.

2. **Group Activity**: Organize students into small groups, and ask each group to create a detailed outline of the text. Students should look at the table of contents but create more fleshed-out outlines showing the parts of the book and the major ideas and details in each part. Students should discuss why Gladwell might have chosen to break the book into those specific chapters and include the case studies at the end. (You may wish to end the lesson here and continue the next day.)

3. **Independent Writing**: Have students spend time looking over the outlines they created in groups. Ask them to write a couple of paragraphs explaining Gladwell's organizational scheme and whether or not they think it was an effective way to organize the book. Students should address the following three questions in their writing.

   - Does Gladwell's structure help the reader understand his points?
   - Does it make his ideas appealing?
   - Does it make his ideas convincing?

4. **Wrap-Up**: Have students share their thoughts with the full class. Ask students to think about other organizational structures Gladwell could have used and whether those structures would have been more or less effective.

Differentiation

For students who need extra support

- Have students begin by analyzing the structure of a chapter rather than the whole book.

For advanced students

- Require a more sophisticated examination of how the author's organization within each chapter supports the organization of the book as a whole.

Assessment

- Evaluate students' writing for evidence that they understood how structure supports meaning and influences readers.

Additional Resources

- This page from the *New York Times* Learning Network describes how to use some *Times* articles to teach text structures: learning.blogs.nytimes.com/2011/12/12/compare-contrast-cause-effect-problem-solution-common-text-types-in-the-times/.

Notes

After implementing the lesson, reflect on what worked and what you would change the next time.

_____

_____

_____

_____

Writing

Part 2

Overview

The Common Core writing standards won't change the basic way you teach writing—through prewriting, drafting, revising, and editing. However, they might lead to changes in the genres you cover. If you haven't been doing so already, make sure you spend plenty of time on argument and informational writing. Those genres require that students use evidence from a variety of sources. Devote time to teaching students how to conduct research, how to evaluate their sources for reliability and credibility, and how to incorporate sources effectively. Those are crucial skills for students to have in college and beyond. Also try to incorporate technology into the writing process. The standards require that students use technology to produce and publish writing. The following list provides additional guidelines for revising your current writing lessons or for creating new ones.

Planning Checklist

When planning a CCSS-based writing lesson, remember these tips:

☐ If you don't already spend a lot of time on argument and informational writing, make it a bigger part of your curriculum. In the middle- and high-school standards, there is a decreased emphasis on narrative writing and an increased focus on argument and informative writing.

☐ Show students that genres often merge—for example, arguments include information. These genres do not always appear in isolation and should not always be taught that way.

☐ When designing writing prompts, consider trying to make them more authentic. Authentic prompts involve topics and issues that students might face in their communities or see in the world around them. Authentic prompts will motivate students because they'll see the real-life purpose of the assignment. Also use authentic audiences, and submit students' work to those audiences; don't have students write just "for the teacher." They will be more motivated to revise and polish their writing when they know that the "outside world" will see it.

☐ Assign a mix of short and long research projects.

☐ Teach students to be aware of audience and adjust their language accordingly. They should understand when to write in a more formal or less formal style.

☐ Consider problem- and project-based learning as a realistic, 21st-century way to teach research and writing. For more on these areas, see Edutopia's Project-Based Learning site: www.edutopia.org/project-based-learning. Also see *Students Taking Charge: Inside the Learner-Active, Technology-Infused Classroom,* by Nancy Sulla (2011, Eye On Education), which contains examples of problem-based learning across the content areas as well as guidelines for designing your own assignments.

☐ Have students use technology to produce and publish writing, as required by the standards. Think of innovative ways that students can produce and publish writing on blogs and wikis and use other online tools so real audiences can read their work.

☐ The Common Core State Standards do not cover teaching students to write poetry, but they do say that you can include it (and other forms of creative writing) if you wish. See the Common Core State Standards, Appendix A, page 23.

☐ Teach argument, not persuasion. The Common Core State Standards draw a distinction between the two.

> A logical argument . . . convinces the audience because of the perceived merit and reasonableness of the claims and proofs offered rather than either the emotions the writing evokes in the audience or the character or credentials of the writer. (Common Core State Standards, p. 24)

Persuasive writing appeals to an audience's emotions. It often depends on techniques such as bandwagon, glittering generalities, name-calling, plain folks, and snob appeal. Argument, on the other hand, appeals to logic and reason, consists of a thesis/claim and supporting evidence, and is usually written in a more formal style. The Common Core says that argument has a "special place" in the standards because it is such a crucial kind of writing to learn for college and careers. Here are some strategies for teaching this genre.

Strategies for Teaching Argument

- Teach concession-refutation. Students should be aware of and address each side of an issue, not just their own side.

- Show students how to avoid common logical errors.

- Analyze mentor texts with students. They can look for examples of concession-refutation in newspapers and magazines and see how the author supports his or her claims with logical, clear evidence.

- Teach students how to marshal facts for their arguments. Students need to learn how to create focused search terms, sort and analyze their search results, assess the credibility and accuracy of their sources, and incorporate their sources effectively.

Lesson Plans at a Glance

Lesson Plan 15   Strengthen Your Argument! Developing
and Distinguishing Your Claims

Lesson Plan 16   Where Do I Begin? Creating a Focused Research Question
Handout—Research Activity Sheet

Lesson Plan 17   Don't Just Google: Using Advanced Search Terms to Find Information
Handout—Which Search Engine Is Best?

Lesson Plan 18   Quote or Paraphrase? How to Incorporate Sources
Handout—Ways to Incorporate Sources

Lesson Plan 19   Collaborate in the Cloud: Contributing to a Class Wiki

Lesson Plan 20   Who's Reading This, Anyway? Describing
Information for Different Audiences

Lesson Plan 21   What Comes Next? Using Colons Effectively

Lesson Plan 22   Reflections of a Writer:
Using Textual Evidence to Support Written Reflection
Handout—Reflections of a Writer: Writing a Reflective Essay

Strengthen Your Argument!

Developing and Distinguishing Your Claims

Lesson Plan 15

Grade Levels: 9–10

Time Frame: Approximately two class periods

Overview: As explained on page 66 of this book, argument writing holds a special place in the Common Core State Standards. This lesson will help students learn how to use evidence strategically when writing an argument. For sample argument writing topics, see Appendix B on page 171 of this book. Use this lesson after students have chosen a topic and begun gathering evidence that they will use when writing.

Common Core State Standards

- 9–10: Writing, Standard 1: Write arguments to support claims in an analysis of substantive topics or texts, using valid reasoning and relevant and sufficient evidence. a. Introduce precise claim(s), distinguish the claim(s) from alternative or opposite claims, and create an organization that establishes clear relationships among claim(s), counterclaims, reasons, and evidence. b. Develop claim(s) and counterclaims fairly, supplying evidence for each while pointing out the strengths and limitations of both in a manner that anticipates the audience's knowledge level and concerns.

Objectives

- Students will introduce claims and distinguish them clearly from opposing claims.

- Students will develop their claims and counterclaims in a way that acknowledges their audiences' needs and concerns.

- Students will organize reasons, evidence, and responses to opposing claims logically in written arguments.

Background Knowledge Required

Students should have gathered their evidence at this point and be tying it into their essays.

Materials Needed

- Students should have their evidence/essay notes with them. Remind them the day before to bring them in.

Agenda

1. **Introduction**: Give students these sample sentences—read them or display them on a board:

   a. Teen curfew laws are just another example of adults trying to take all the fun out of being a teenager.

   b. Teen curfew laws have good intentions—to keep teens safe. However, teens and their families should be trusted to make their own decisions about when a teen should come home at night.

   Have students vote on which one is the most convincing. Ask them to justify their votes. Discuss what makes the second argument the most convincing (not length). It's effective because it doesn't ignore the other person's argument; it addresses the opposing argument and points out why it is invalid. An argument also needs to be fair—just insulting another person/audience (argument 1) makes an opposing argument less fair and therefore less convincing.

2. **Independent Work**: Have students look at the research they've gathered and the evidence they have to support their arguments. Ask students to make T-charts listing possible opposing claims on the left and ways to address those claims on the right.

3. **Partner Work**: Organize students into pairs. The writer of the T-chart reads the refutations of the opposing claims (the column on the right), and the partner looks for holes in the writer's thinking or places where there is not enough information to satisfy the intended audience. The partner should help the writer consider these questions: How much does the audience already know on the topic? Does the treatment of counterclaims sufficiently address any concerns the audience might have on the topic? Then the students switch roles and repeat the exercise. (Note: You may wish to break the lesson here and continue the next day.)

4. **Wrap-Up**: Have students incorporate their work from the lesson into their essay drafts. Students should write one or two sentences explaining how they strengthened their writing and submit them to you. Alternatively, students could read their sentences to a small group or share them in the full class.

Extend the Lesson

- Ask students to exchange drafts with a partner. Pass out copies of the 4-point rubric that follows. Ask students to read their partners' drafts carefully and to score them based on the rubric. After that, students should meet with their partners to discuss and explain how they arrived at the scores.

- You can also have students find additional examples of effective concession-refutation in local newspapers.

Differentiation

For students who need extra support

- Have students write argumentative paragraphs with one or two reasons and evidence before they do full essays; that will give them more practice in describing evidence.

For advanced students

- Require that students include at least four reasons with evidence for each reason and also refute two or three opposing claims.

Assessment

- Monitor students as they complete the partner work. Check to make sure that each T-chart has two or three opposing claims with corresponding responses/refutations. If students are having a hard time finding holes in their partners' thinking, suggest that they instead explain why the response/refutation is so strong that they can't find holes.

- Use the following rubric to evaluate students' essay drafts.

Score 4.0	The student - Introduces a claim about the topic. - Includes at least three reasons or pieces of evidence to support the claim. - Acknowledges alternative or opposing claims. No major errors or omissions in the score 4.0 content.
Score 3.5	The student demonstrates success at the 3.0 level plus partial success at the 4.0 level.
Score 3.0	The student - Introduces a claim about the topic. - Includes one or two reasons or pieces of evidence to support the claim. - Acknowledges alternative or opposing claims but in an unfair or illogical way (e.g., by insulting the opposition or by acknowledging an irrelevant claim). No major errors or omissions in the score 3.0 content.
Score 2.5	The student demonstrates success at the 2.0 level plus partial success at the 3.0 level.
Score 2.0	The student - Introduces a claim about the topic. - Includes one or two reasons or pieces of evidence to support the claim. No major errors or omissions in the score 2.0 content.
Score 1.5	The student demonstrates partial success at the 2.0 level; the student's claim may be implied rather than stated; the supporting reasons may be only loosely related to the topic.
Score 1.0	With help, the student achieves partial success at score 2.0 and 3.0 contents.
Score 0.5	With help, the student achieves partial success at score 2.0 content but not score 3.0 content.
Score 0.0	Even with help, the student has no success.

Additional Resources

This page from ReadWriteThink offers a detailed 4-point rubric for evaluating persuasive writing: www.readwritethink.org/files/resources/printouts/Persuasion%20Rubric .pdf. It is titled Persuasion Rubric but applies well to argument writing.

Notes

After implementing the lesson, reflect on what worked and what you would change the next time.

_____

_____

_____

_____

Where Do I Begin?

Creating a Focused Research Question

Grade Levels: 9–12

Time Frame: Approximately two class periods

Overview: In this lesson, students conduct short, informational research projects. The Common Core State Standards emphasize the importance of having students engage in a variety of short and longer research so they learn to become independent thinkers and gatherers of information. This lesson focuses on informational writing but can also be used with argument writing because that genre similarly requires research. You may want to involve science teachers in this lesson.

Common Core State Standards

- 9–10: Writing, Standard 2: Write informative/explanatory texts to examine and convey complex ideas, concepts, and information clearly and accurately through the effective selection, organization, and analysis of content.

- 11–12: Writing, Standard 2: Write informative/explanatory texts to examine and convey complex ideas, concepts, and information clearly and accurately through the effective selection, organization, and analysis of content.

- 9–10: Writing, Standard 4: Produce clear and coherent writing in which the development, organization, and style are appropriate to task, purpose, and audience.

- 9–10: Writing, Standard 7: Conduct short as well as more sustained research projects to answer a question (including a self-generated question) or solve a problem; narrow or broaden the inquiry when appropriate; synthesize multiple sources on the subject, demonstrating understanding of the subject under investigation.

- 11–12: Writing, Standard 4: Produce clear and coherent writing in which the development, organization, and style are appropriate to task, purpose, and audience.

- 11–12: Writing, Standard 7: Conduct short as well as more sustained research projects to answer a question (including a self-generated question) or solve a problem; narrow or broaden the inquiry when appropriate; synthesize multiple sources on the subject, demonstrating understanding of the subject under investigation.

Objectives

- Each student will write a focused research question.

- Students will research multiple sources to answer their research questions, refocusing the question as necessary.

Background Knowledge Required

No particular background knowledge is required for this lesson.

Materials Needed

- Copies of the handout: Research Activity Sheet, p. 77

Agenda

1. **Introduction**: Have students create authentic problems to research, based on something they are learning in science class. For example, how might scientists attempt to slow global warming? There is no one right answer to this question, so it allows students to do research and make discoveries rather than simply regurgitate something they were taught.

2. **Full-Class Focusing Activity**: Explain that with any topic, the possibilities for research are practically endless. Therefore, a good research project must be focused. That means narrowing the field of research to a manageable size. Tell students to ask the following questions:

   - What is my purpose for writing?
   - Who is my audience?
   - What guidelines did my teacher (or boss or editor, etc.) give me?

   For example, if you use the global warming example, ask students to consider how their question would change if they were presenting information to a group of scientists vs. presenting information to policy makers vs. presenting information to younger students trying to understand global warming. Assign or have students choose an audience for their research (You may allow students to choose different audiences, or you may have the class agree on one audience to whom all students will address their writing.) Also decide on the format you would like students to use when presenting their information (essay, web page, oral report, etc.)

3. **Small-Group Research**: Organize students into small groups, distribute the handout, and have the members of each group collaborate to complete part 1.

4. **Homework**: Have students work independently to complete part 2 of the handout.

5. **Small-Group Activity** (next class period): In class, have students meet with their research groups. Remind them that, just as they had to focus their research topics to make them manageable, now they need to focus their research findings to make the material manageable.

   - Students should review their research findings and decide which facts and details are most useful for creating strong answers to their research questions.
   - They should use their focused findings to create outlines for their essays, web pages, or reports.
   - Each group should submit a copy of its outline to you.

6. **Homework**: Each group should write its essays, web pages, or report, following the guidelines for length and format that you specify. In addition, each group should supply a works-cited page. If time allows, you may choose to have students complete the work in class, the better to facilitate gathering in groups.

7. **Wrap-Up**: Have groups share their research with the full class. Then ask volunteers to share helpful tips for researching an informational topic. They may offer suggestions about using focused search terms in a web browser, asking a librarian for help, eliminating unreliable sources, etc.

Extend the Lesson

- Teach the proper format for creating a works-cited page (see Lesson Plan 31 on page 146).

Differentiation

For students who need extra support

- Allow students to work with their groups or partners from their groups to complete part 2 of the handout.

For advanced students

- When assigning students to groups, consider grouping advanced students in pairs or threes so that each student carries a greater responsibility for completing the work.

- Schedule a brief discussion time to follow each small-group activity. Ask volunteers to give examples of how they completed a task. Use their responses as an opportunity to troubleshoot problems that struggling students may be having.

Assessment

- Check each group's research question to make sure it is focused and relevant to the assignment. If necessary, ask groups to narrow their focus (perhaps by using a proper noun instead of a general term).

- While small groups evaluate their research findings, monitor their discussions. Watch for examples of reliable, solid, or well-targeted research and share them with the class.

- Review each group's outline. Check for the proper format of introduction, body paragraph, and conclusion. If necessary, have students revise their outlines in response to your feedback (e.g., arrange information in a logical order; eliminate weak, vague, or redundant points; cut the outline down to size per the length requirement).

- Assess each group's paragraph/section and works-cited list using the following rubric.

Score 4.0	The group • Writes a focused, informative piece of the web page. • Uses relevant ideas, facts, details, and/or examples. • Selects information appropriate for its audience. • Arranges the paragraph's topic sentence and information logically. • Cites reliable sources of information. No major errors or omissions in the score 4.0 content.
Score 3.5	The group demonstrates success at the 3.0 level plus partial success at the 4.0 level.
Score 3.0	The group • Writes an informative piece of the web page, but it lacks a tight focus. • Uses ideas, facts, details, and/or examples, but one or two are vague, irrelevant, or redundant. • Arranges sentences logically, with one or two exceptions. • Cites sources of information but includes an unreliable source. No major errors or omissions in the score 3.0 content.
Score 2.5	The group demonstrates success at the 2.0 level plus partial success at the 3.0 level.
Score 2.0	The group • Writes a piece of the web page that does not clearly connect to the class's outline OR uses a predominantly persuasive or narrative approach. • Offers too few supporting details OR details that are vague, irrelevant, or redundant. • Arranges sentences in a mostly random manner. • Cites no sources of information. No major errors or omissions in the score 2.0 content.
Score 1.5	The group demonstrates partial success at the 2.0 level.
Score 1.0	With help, the group achieves partial success at score 2.0 and 3.0 contents.
Score 0.5	With help, the group achieves partial success at score 2.0 content but not score 3.0 content.
Score 0.0	Even with help, the group has no success.

Additional Resources

- The Purdue Online Writing Lab has helpful pages on these topics:
  - Conducting research: owl.english.purdue.edu/owl/section/2/8
  - Using MLA format to create a works-cited page: owl.english.purdue.edu/owl/section/2/11

Notes

After implementing the lesson, reflect on what worked and what you would change the next time.

_____

_____

_____

_____

Research Activity Sheet

Part 1: Complete the table below.

1. Write your research question. _____ _____	
2. List search terms (words and phrases) that will help you find information to answer your research question. Your search terms: ▪ ▪ ▪ ▪ ▪	**3.** Once you perform a few searches, focus your search terms. Your focused search terms: ▪ ▪ ▪ ▪ ▪

Part 2: Carry out your research by completing each item below.

1. Perform a search for information in at least *two* different formats. For example, search for websites and search for books. List three to five reliable sources below, and write a brief note about how each source can help answer your research question.

Source	How It Is Helpful
Source 1	
Source 2	
Source 3	
Source 4	
Source 5	

2. Check off each task below as you complete it.

- Review the research question in Part 1, item 1.
- Review the sources you found in item 1, above, and put stars by the *two* sources that would best help answer the research question.
- Gather useful facts and ideas from each starred source by taking notes, marking up printouts or photocopies, or attaching and writing on sticky notes.
- Take this work with you to class to help complete the next part of your research assignment.

Don't Just Google

Using Advanced Search Terms to Find Information

Grade Levels: 9–12

Time Frame: Approximately one class period

Overview: In this lesson, students learn how to use advanced searches to produce better results when conducting research. Most students know how to type something into Google and even use a variety of search terms, but many students are not familiar with more advanced search methods.

Common Core State Standards

- 9–10: Writing, Standard 8: Gather relevant information from multiple authoritative print and digital sources, using advanced searches effectively; assess the usefulness of each source in answering the research question; integrate information into the text selectively to maintain the flow of ideas, avoiding plagiarism and following a standard format for citation.

- 11–12: Writing, Standard 8: Gather relevant information from multiple authoritative print and digital sources, using advanced searches effectively; assess the strengths and limitations of each source in terms of the task, purpose, and audience; integrate information into the text selectively to maintain the flow of ideas, avoiding plagiarism and overreliance on any one source and following a standard format for citation.

Objectives

- Students will perform advanced searches online.

Background Knowledge Required

Students should be beginning an informational essay on an assigned or a self-selected topic.

Materials Needed

- Copies of the handout: Which Search Engine Is Best?, p. 82

Agenda

1. **Introduction**: Ask students what methods they use for formulating search terms when researching information. "Do you put terms in quotation marks? Do you try a variety of word combinations? Have you ever used an advanced search?" Discuss.

Tell students that the purpose of today's lesson is to help them conduct more efficient research so that they get better results the first time.

2. **Mini-Lesson**: Teach students about three things that will help them conduct more effective research: advanced searches, search operators, and choosing the right browser.

   - Ask students if they have ever used Google's advanced search feature, available here: www.google.ca/advanced_search. Complete the form with students using a sample topic or a topic they've been researching in class.
   - Show students how to use search operators, such as the ones available here: http://support.google.com/websearch/bin/answer.py?hl=en&p=adv_operators &answer=136861. For example, they can put a dash before a word to exclude all results containing that word. They can use a tilde before a word to include that word plus its synonyms.
   - Tell students that there might be times they don't want to use Google. For example, if they are looking for a science news article, they might want to use a science news database rather than a very general browser. For example, science .gov searches 55 databases and more than 2,100 government-run science websites; students can use that search engine if they are looking for authoritative information on a current science topic. SweetSearch is a search engine designed specifically for students. The sites have been evaluated ahead of time, so students are less likely to get spammy, irrelevant results. Show students some possible databases and other kinds of browsers, and see if they are already familiar with any of them. Have students find out about other kinds of search engines and databases on their own.

3. **Practice**: Have students try using search operators and advanced search forms when they gather information for an essay they are writing in class. Also have them consult a variety of search engines. Distribute the handout, and have students complete it.

Differentiation

For students who need extra support

- Focus on fewer search operators at a time, and give students more practice with each one.

For advanced students

- Allow students to practice with more complex search operators.

Assessment

- Evaluate students' work on the handout that follows.

- In the future, when students gather information for essays, you can have them submit a notes page on how they researched their topic, and you can assess that along with assessing their writing.

Additional Resources

- Calishain, Tara, and Rael Dornfest. *Google Hacks: Tips & Tools for Smarter Searching.* 2nd edition. Sebastopol, CA: O'Reilly Media, 2004. This book is listed as an exemplar text in Appendix B of the Common Core State Standards.

Notes

After implementing the lesson, reflect on what worked and what you would change the next time.

_____

_____

_____

_____

Which Search Engine Is Best?

As you conduct research, make notes of which engines you used and what kinds of results you found.

Search Engine	Types of Results the Search Engine Produced	Did the Results Meet My Research Needs? Explain.

Quote or Paraphrase?

How to Incorporate Sources

Grade Levels: 9–12

Time Frame: Approximately one or two class periods

Overview: This lesson will help students understand when to paraphrase, when to quote, and how to avoid plagiarism. Students will also learn how to incorporate quotations into a text and how to make sure they don't rely too much on any one source, as required by the grades 11 and 12 CCSS. Use this lesson during a unit on research-based informational/explanatory or argument writing, once students have gathered sources but have not begun drafting.

Common Core State Standards

- 9–10: Writing, Standard 8: Gather relevant information from multiple authoritative print and digital sources, using advanced searches effectively; assess the usefulness of each source in answering the research question; integrate information into the text selectively to maintain the flow of ideas, avoiding plagiarism and following a standard format for citation.

- 11–12: Writing, Standard 8: Gather relevant information from multiple authoritative print and digital sources, using advanced searches effectively; assess the strengths and limitations of each source in terms of the task, purpose, and audience; integrate information into the text selectively to maintain the flow of ideas, avoiding plagiarism and overreliance on any one source and following a standard format for citation.

Objectives

- Students will learn to make decisions about whether to paraphrase or to quote.

- Students will understand what constitutes plagiarism and learn what paraphrasing really means.

- Students will practice incorporating quotations into their writing.

Background Knowledge Required

Students should have experience conducting research and recording where they find their information. They should have some familiarity with incorporating quotes and paraphrasing information.

Materials Needed

- Copies of the handout: Ways to Incorporate Sources, p. 86

Agenda

1. **Review**: Tell students that in previous grades, they probably heard the terms *paraphrase* and *plagiarize*. Ask students to define each term and to consider when they might want to paraphrase information, when they might need to quote it, and why that would matter to readers. Mention that general, common-sense info does not need to be quoted. Ask why it's important to not rely on any one source. Caution students that using too many sources may make their writing seem too scholarly and inaccessible, depending on the audience and purpose. When discussing paraphrasing, reinforce that changing only a word or two constitutes plagiarism. You may want to have a serious conversation with students about the repercussions of plagiarism, not just at your school but in the real world, too. Emphasize to students that when they paraphrase, they should alter sentence structure, consider which words are replaceable, combine sentences, and decide what to leave out and what to keep from the original. Also discuss the importance of citing sources. (See Lesson Plan 31 for teaching MLA style.)

2. **Independent Work**: Give students the handout. Have students complete it using the sources they've gathered for their essays. (Note: You may wish to end the lesson here and continue the next day.)

3. **Full-Class Discussion**: Go over the handout as a full class or have students share their handouts with a partner.

4. **Wrap-Up**: Require students to include a mix of paraphrased and quoted information when they draft their essays.

Differentiation

For students who need extra support

- Give them easier passages to paraphrase, and help them practice summarizing information from a source.

For advanced students

- Have them work with information from more complex sources.

Assessment

- Evaluate students' handouts to see whether they effectively paraphrased and explained quotations.

- Make sure that students continue to practice these skills throughout the year. When you assess students' writing, include incorporating sources on the rubrics you use.

Additional Resources

- This page provides additional practice on quoting, paraphrasing, and summarizing: owl.english.purdue.edu/owl/resource/563/01.

- The University of Houston at Victoria has a helpful guide to deciding when to quote, paraphrase, or summarize: www.uhv.edu/ac/style/pdf/quote.pdf.

- This page provides examples of successful and unsuccessful paraphrases: writing.wisc .edu/Handbook/QPA_paraphrase.html.

Notes

After implementing the lesson, reflect on what worked and what you would change the next time.

_____

_____

_____

_____

Ways to Incorporate Sources

Choose one of the sources you're using for your essay. Use that source to complete the following exercises.

1. **Paraphrasing**: Paraphrasing shows your understanding of the content. Make sure to paraphrase fully by changing the wording and sentence structures. Don't replace just one or two words here or there. If you don't know what a word means, don't blindly include it in your paraphrase. Look it up and put it in your own words rather than putting it in a paraphrase that has no meaning to you.

   Pick a sentence from your source and paraphrase it below.

   _____

   _____

   _____

2. **Summarizing**: Summarizing also shows your understanding of the content.

   In the space below, summarize something from your source.

   _____

   _____

   _____

3. **Quoting**: Quoting is useful when you want to be able to use the author's expertise. It is also good to quote when the author's wording is clever or catchy and paraphrasing it wouldn't have the same impact. Be careful not to quote too often, though; it can bog down your essay. You should also be careful not to throw the quotes into your essay; make sure you provide context and explain them.

   Pick something to quote from the article, and write it below. Include a sentence or two of your own to introduce the quote, and a sentence or two to summarize the quote.

   _____

   _____

   _____

   _____

   _____

Collaborate in the Cloud

Contributing to a Class Wiki

Grade Levels: 9–12

Time Frame: Approximately one class period

Overview: The Common Core State Standards require that students use technology in a variety of ways when writing—not just to conduct research and publish writing but also to collaborate with others and update content as needed. In this lesson, students will create a wiki together that they will use to gather and update information for an argument they are writing.

Common Core State Standards

- 9–10: Writing, Standard 6: Use technology, including the Internet, to produce, publish, and update individual or shared writing products, taking advantage of technology's capacity to link to other information and to display information flexibly and dynamically.

- 11–12: Writing, Standard 6: Use technology, including the Internet, to produce, publish, and update individual or shared writing products in response to ongoing feedback, including new arguments or information.

- 9–10: Writing Standard 9: Draw evidence from literary or informational texts to support analysis, reflection, and research.

- 11–12: Writing, Standard 9: Draw evidence from literary or informational texts to support analysis, reflection, and research.

Objectives

- Students will contribute relevant information (including linked content) to a class wiki.

- Students will update content on the class wiki as necessary.

Background Knowledge Required

Students should be in the beginning stages of an argument essay. They should have a topic but not have done much research yet. (See Appendix B on page 171 for sample argument writing prompts.)

Before using this lesson, you should set up the class wiki. Choose a school-friendly wiki site, such as PBworks, Wetpaint, or Wikispaces. Add categories to the wiki, such as these: evidence, analysis, counterclaims.

Materials Needed

- Computers with access to the wiki you have set up

Agenda

1. **Introduction**: Ask students to spend a minute writing down some thoughts about the benefits and drawbacks of collaborative writing (people contributing to a wiki, for example). Have some students share their responses. Tell students that they are going to contribute to a wiki to collaborate on their argument essays. Each student will be responsible for contributing some research to the wiki.

2. **Independent Work**: Ask students to contribute one or two items to each category of the wiki. They should choose their contributions with the ultimate goal of helping one another collect the most accurate information possible and hyperlink their contributions as appropriate.

3. **Partner Activity**: After students contribute individually to the wiki, organize them into pairs to review, add to, and edit other people's contributions. Go over class rules for editing one another's sections respectfully.

4. **Wrap-Up**: Have students reflect on their experience creating the wiki. They should refer to the notes they jotted at the beginning of the lesson to see how their ideas changed. How was this method of collaborating more or less helpful than a class discussion or another way of comparing information during the brainstorming stage of writing?

Differentiation

For students who need extra support

- Provide more brainstorming time so students can flesh out their answers. Pair students who are more tech-savvy with those who are less tech-savvy so they can help each other.

For advanced students

- Have students contribute content to additional sections of the wiki.

- Require that students use graphics and other visuals to enhance their wiki entries. Discuss the importance of visuals to teach and not just to decorate.

Assessment

- Evaluate students' contributions to their own sections of the wiki as well as their edits or additions to the other sections.

- You may want to create a rubric for evaluating wikis (with students' assistance) and make sure students are familiar with it before they begin writing. Categories could include thoroughness of content, accessibility of the language, and correct use of mechanics.

Additional Resources

- This page suggests fun ways to use wikis in the classroom: www.smartteaching .org/blog/2008/08/50-ways-to-use-wikis-for-a-more-collaborative-and-interactive -classroom.

- The Cool Cat Teacher Blog provides tips and ideas for using wikis in your lessons: coolcatteacher.blogspot.com/2005/12/wiki-wiki-teaching-art-of-using-wiki.html.

Notes

After implementing the lesson, reflect on what worked and what you would change the next time.

_____

_____

_____

_____

Who's Reading This, Anyway?

Describing Information for Different Audiences

Grade Levels: 9–12

Time Frame: Approximately one class period

Overview: In this lesson, students will learn to consider their audience when making writing decisions. Students will practice adjusting language and word choices to suit different audiences and purposes.

Common Core State Standards

- 9–10: Writing, Standard 2: Write informative/explanatory texts to examine and convey complex ideas, concepts, and information clearly and accurately through the effective selection, organization, and analysis of content. d. Use precise language and domain-specific vocabulary to manage the complexity of the topic. e. Establish and maintain a formal style and objective tone while attending to the norms and conventions of the discipline in which they are writing.

- 11–12: Writing, Standard 2: Write informative/explanatory texts to examine and convey complex ideas, concepts, and information clearly and accurately through the effective selection, organization, and analysis of content. d. Use precise language, domain-specific vocabulary, and techniques such as metaphor, simile, and analogy to manage the complexity of the topic. e. Establish and maintain a formal style and objective tone while attending to the norms and conventions of the discipline in which they are writing.

Objectives

- Students will adjust their word choices, sentence structures, and tone for different audiences.

- Students will write in different styles for audiences with different levels of background knowledge on a topic.

Background Knowledge Required

Use this lesson toward the beginning of an informational writing unit. Students should not have done any drafting at this point.

Materials Needed

- Students' notes for their informational essays. Remind them the day before to bring them in.

Agenda

1. **Introduction**: Tell students that today, the class will discuss audience. Ask them to think about how their informational writing might change based on their audience. Have them spend a few minutes jotting down some possible responses.

2. **Mini-Lesson**: Ask students to imagine that they are experts on tornadoes (or some other topic of your choosing). How would they present that information differently to

   - elementary-school kids?
   - other experts on tornadoes?
   - residents of a town where a tornado hit?
   - residents of an area where tornadoes rarely hit?

   Write all four possible audiences on the board. Discuss as a class how the tone and the amount of background knowledge a writer provides would vary depending on the audience's experience with the topic. For example, elementary-school kids would need a basic definition of a tornado with examples and visuals. Other tornado experts would not need such a definition; that could seem condescending. The writing could include sophisticated language and terms used without definitions. You may wish to discuss the differences among Tier One (everyday), Two (academic), and Three (domain-specific) words.

   Residents in an area where tornadoes often threaten would be familiar with tornado safety, but most probably are not scientists, so writing would need to be very clear and include explanations of terms used. A writer would have to be even clearer when writing for residents in areas that never experience tornadoes; they have even less familiarity with the topic. Tell students that level of experience is not the only factor to consider. They also have to consider context. Is the audience hearing this info on *Good Morning America* or reading about it in the *New York Times*, in a scientific journal, or on a student's blog? Are audience members young or old?

3. **Independent Work**: Assign students two different audiences for the informational essays they are working on in class. Have them write sample paragraphs for each audience, considering the elements you discussed as a class.

4. **Wrap-Up**: Have students discuss and/or write reflections on what they did differently for each version. Then assign the audience that students will ultimately use when they draft their full essays, or allow them to choose the one that they prefer and write their full essays for that audience.

Extend the Lesson

- Ask students to gather a bunch of articles on the same topic from different kinds of publications for different audiences. Give them guidelines about where to find such articles. Students should write brief analyses of how each source presents information for that publication's audience. They should use specific examples from each source.

- When students complete their drafts, have them work with partners to review one another's work and make sure that the language and tone for the chosen audience are consistent throughout the essays.

Differentiation

For students who need extra support

- Spend more time helping students with word choice and language decisions for various audiences.

For advanced students

- Require that students use even more domain-specific (Tier Three) words in their essays.

Assessment

- Evaluate whether students' essays demonstrate an awareness of audience, as evidenced by their language, word choices, and tone. Make sure to include audience awareness on the rubric you use to assess their essays.

- Check students' reflections for understanding of how writing changes based on audience.

Additional Resources

- This page from Colorado State University provides a helpful list of questions to consider when analyzing audience: writing.colostate.edu/guides/processes/audmod/com2c2.cfm.

Notes

After implementing the lesson, reflect on what worked and what you would change the next time.

_____

_____

_____

_____

What Comes Next?

Using Colons Effectively

Grade Levels: 9–10; can also be done in grades 11 and 12 as a review

Time Frame: Approximately one class period

Overview: In this lesson, students learn the rules for proper colon use and then apply them to their own writing. This lesson can be done along with Lesson Plan 18 on incorporating sources.

Common Core State Standards

- 9–10: Writing, Standard 5: Develop and strengthen writing as needed by planning, revising, editing, rewriting, or trying a new approach, focusing on addressing what is most significant for a specific purpose and audience.

- 9–10: Language, Standard 2: Demonstrate command of the conventions of standard English capitalization, punctuation, and spelling when writing. b. Use a colon to introduce a list or quotation.

Objectives

- Students will learn how to use a colon to introduce a list, to introduce a quotation, and to emphasize a key point.

- Students will incorporate colons into their own writing.

Background Knowledge Required

Students should be familiar with basic punctuation and with quoting effectively from sources.

Materials Needed

- Students should bring in drafts of essays they are writing for class. Remind them the day before.

Agenda

1. **Introduction**: Tell students that today, they'll look closely at a sophisticated form of punctuation: the colon. Ask students what they already know about colons.

2. **Mini-Lesson**: Show students three examples of colon usage, and have them figure out the purpose of each one. Here are three examples you can use.

Example 1: In *On Writing Well* (1998), William Zinsser explains that American writing is too cluttered. According to Zinsser, writers should do the following:

> Consider all the prepositions that are draped onto verbs that don't need any help. We no longer head committees. We head them up. We don't face problems anymore. We face up to them when we can free up a few minutes. A small detail, you may say—not worth bothering about. It *is* worth bothering about. Writing improves in direct ration to the number of things we can keep out of it that shouldn't be there. (p. 13)

Why is a colon necessary there? (*Answer: To introduce a quotation.*)

Example 2: Effective writing includes these key qualities:

- A clear organizational structure
- Precise language
- Details and examples
- Proper use of grammar and conventions

Why is a colon necessary there? (*Answer: To introduce a list of items.*)

Explain to students that a colon is usually unnecessary after a verb. For example, if you were to write, "My list includes apples, bananas, and oranges," you would not include a colon after *includes*, whether the list was bulleted or within the sentence.

The word before the colon should be what the list is about. For example, in the list in example 2 you wouldn't write, "These qualities are important to consider:" because the list isn't about considering, it's about the qualities.

Example 3: You can see my point: proper punctuation matters!

Why does a colon work there? (*Answer: To show that the second sentence closely explains the first one.*)

If a colon is within a sentence, the first word following the colon is lowercased unless it's a proper noun. If a colon introduces two or more sentences, a direct question, or a quotation, then the first word following the colon is capitalized.

3. **Independent Writing**: Tell students that each example represents an important colon rule. Have them look at their writing and see if they've used colons correctly. (They can swap essays with partners or look at their own writing.) They should correct colons as necessary. If they haven't used a colon as in example 3, they should try adding one for practice.

Extend the Lesson

- Introduce em dashes and discuss when they can be used in place of colons and/or parentheses within sentences.

Differentiation

For students who need extra support

- Focus on only one colon rule at a time, such as using a colon to introduce a quotation. Give students extra practice with that rule.

For advanced students

- Students can play around with the third example of colon use, which is more sophisticated than the other two.

Assessment

- Include proper use of colons in the rubric you use to assess students' essays.

- Follow up on this lesson throughout the year as students do other kinds of writing in class.

Additional Resources

- Grammar Girl has this helpful guide to using colons correctly: http://grammar.quickanddirtytips.com/colon-grammar.aspx.

Notes

After implementing the lesson, reflect on what worked and what you would change the next time.

_____

_____

_____

_____

Reflections of a Writer

Using Textual Evidence to Support Written Reflection

Grade Levels: 9–12

Time Frame: Approximately one class period

Overview: In this lesson, students use a written format to reflect on what they learned from a work of literature or an informational text. Use this lesson in conjunction with one of the reading lessons that emphasize close textual analysis or answering text-based questions. Examples are Lessons Plans 1, 3, 4, 5, 7, and 8.

Common Core State Standards
- 9–12: Writing, Standard 9: Draw evidence from literary or informational texts to support analysis, reflection, and research. a. Apply *[grade-level] Reading standards* to literature. b. Apply *[grade-level] Reading standards* to literary nonfiction.

- 9–12: Writing, Standard 10: Write routinely over extended time frames (time for research, reflection, and revision) and shorter time frames (a single sitting or a day or two) for a range of tasks, purposes, and audiences.

Objectives
- Students will use textual evidence to support, clarify, and strengthen a reflective writing piece.

Background Knowledge Required
This lesson builds on a reading lesson of your choice that students previously completed in your class.

Materials Needed
- Students' notes from a previous reading lesson (that you specify) and the associated literature or informational text. Remind them the day before to bring them in.

- Copies of the handout: Reflections of a Writer: Writing a Reflective Essay, p. 99

Agenda
1. **Introduction**: Write the following words in a list on the board: *reflect, reflects, reflecting, reflective.* Ask students to play "word association" by jotting down five to ten words that come to mind in response to the words you listed. Then have volunteers read their lists, explaining connections if necessary. Make sure that the word *reflect* is defined not just as "to give back an image" but also as "to think seriously." Use

students' ideas of mirrors and other types of reflections to bring the conversation around to reflective writing. Ask questions such as these:

- What purpose might reflective writing serve in an academic setting?
- Whose ideas are at the center of the reflective writing?
- What forms might reflective writing take? (e.g., personal essay, journal entry, blog entry)
- Who might be the audience for reflective writing?

2. **Writing Task**: Have students take out their notes from a particular lesson that the class completed recently. First, they should read their notes, using them to remember what they learned, what ideas captured their attention, and what questions the material raised. Second, they should take out the literature or informational text they used with the lesson and skim it to refresh their memories. Finally, each student should complete the handout, which includes the writing task and topic ideas.

3. **Wrap-Up**: Take a poll to find out which formats and audiences students selected for their reflective writing pieces. Collect students' writing.

Differentiation

For students who need extra support

- Before assigning the writing task, give a mini-lesson explaining the weaker and stronger traits of reflective writing (see the assessment checklist that follows). Give students copies of the checklist.

For advanced students

- Before assigning the writing task, review elements of personal writing style, such as diction (word choices, from simple to sophisticated; consider connotation as well as denotation); syntax (ways of structuring sentences; rhythm and flow of writing); and tone (the attitude toward the topic that comes through as the personality of the writer). Encourage students to write with awareness and purpose in regard to these qualities.

Assessment

- Though reflective writing is meant to be a form of self-assessment, it is nevertheless a form of writing that can benefit from critique, revision, and practice of the art. This checklist can help you help your students identify areas of strength and weakness in this form of writing.

Traits of Weak Reflective Writing	Traits of Strong Reflective Writing
- Lists isolated facts about the lesson or text.	- Shows how parts of the lesson or text contributed to growth as a writer or scholar.
- Exhibits few or no connections between ideas or observations about the topic of reflection; organization seems random.	- Logically connects ideas or observations using signal words or explanations of how one idea builds upon a previous one.

Traits of Weak Reflective Writing	Traits of Strong Reflective Writing
▪ Demonstrates little analysis or insight.	▪ Shows the impact of the lesson or text through rich analysis or insight.
▪ Shows little or no awareness of audience.	▪ Vocabulary, tone, and choice of evidence show a careful consideration of a target audience.
▪ Shows little or no awareness of the purpose of reflective writing. The piece is a generic narrative or collection of statements.	▪ Demonstrates a clear purpose for choosing the ideas and details in the piece (e.g., to answer a specific question or respond to a writing prompt).
▪ Uses a generic form.	▪ Shows awareness of the tone and structure of a specific form, such as a blog entry, personal essay, or writer's notebook entry.
▪ The purpose of the writing, if evident, conflicts with the form chosen for the writing.	▪ The form of the writing shows careful consideration of the purpose and audience for the piece.
▪ Presents a generic report of a learning experience that could have been written by anyone who had been present in the class.	▪ Presents an individualized report of a learning experience, shaped by the ideas and responses of the writer as a unique person.

Additional Resources

The Kentucky Department of Education has an extensive collection of resources to help teachers teach, model, and assess reflective writing. In an Internet search engine, use the search term *reflective writing Kentucky department of education.*

Notes

After implementing the lesson, reflect on what worked and what you would change the next time.

_____

_____

_____

_____

Reflections of a Writer

Writing a Reflective Essay

Complete each item below.

1. What work of literature or informational text is the subject of your reflective writing?

   _____

   _____

   _____ .

2. What form do you want your reflective writing to take? Ideas include, but aren't limited to, an entry in a writer's journal, a blog entry, and a personal essay. Write your decision here:

   _____

   _____

   _____ .

3. Who will be the audience for your reflective writing? Ideas include, but aren't limited to, yourself (private), your classmates, your teacher, and a public community of interested readers. Write your decision here:

   _____

   _____

   _____ .

4. What main question or idea will give focus to this piece of reflective writing? Choose one or more ideas in the bulleted list below, and check them. On your own paper, respond to the writing prompt, including the part about using evidence from the text to support and explain your ideas.

Choose one or more of the following topics to respond to in writing	and
<ul><li>What suggestions would you give other students on ways to get the most out of this text?</li><li>What was the most useful or meaningful thing you learned from the text?</li><li>What did you learn that seems the most believable in relation to your personal experience? What is the connection between what you learned and your personal experience?</li><li>What big idea did the lesson or text spark in your mind? Write as much as you can about this big idea, including how it connects to the text.</li><li>What part of the lesson or text surprised you or confused you? Explain your reaction.</li><li>In what way(s) have you grown as a reader and/or writer in response to studying this text?</li><li>What strategies did you use to participate in class effectively and to complete assignments to the best of your ability? What would you do differently if you had the chance?</li><li>What else would you like to learn about the text, its ideas, its author, or other aspects of the lesson?</li></ul>	use evidence from the work of literature or informational text to support your ideas. *Evidence* includes details, examples, reasons, direct quotations, paraphrased ideas, and summaries of main ideas or paragraphs or entire texts.

Speaking and Listening

Part 3

Overview

The days of having students give presentations with index cards are long gone. Students need practice using technology when they present, as they will be required to do in college and their careers. They should "make strategic use of digital media and visual displays of data to express information and enhance understanding of presentations" (Common Core State Standards, p. 48). The standards also require students to engage in a variety of small- and large-group discussions. Students must learn how to listen and respond to one another effectively and how to disagree respectfully and build from one another's ideas. For more suggestions on teaching speaking and listening, read the following checklist.

Planning Checklist

When planning a CCSS-based speaking and listening lesson, remember these tips:

☐ Provide opportunities for students to read aloud so they can develop fluency and practice adjusting the pace, accuracy, tone, and stress with which they read.

☐ Students should deliver presentations for a variety of purposes. They should incorporate media and visuals into their presentations and make sure that their content and language are appropriate for their particular audience.

☐ Teach listening skills by having students listen to audio or film versions of texts. Students should compare what they gain from reading a text to what they gain from hearing the audio or film version. Students should also listen to speeches and evaluate the speakers' points of view and use of rhetoric and evidence.

☐ Make sure that you begin text-based class discussions by having students look closely at the words and language. Don't jump too quickly into broad or opinion-based questions until you're sure that students have a clear understanding of the work itself. The authors of the Common Core explain that an effective discussion starts with focused questions.

> An effective set of discussion questions might begin with relatively simple questions requiring attention to specific words, details, and arguments and then move on to explore the impact of those specifics on the text as a whole. Good questions will often linger over specific phrases and sentences to ensure careful

comprehension and also promote deep thinking and substantive analysis of the text. . . . Often, curricula surrounding texts leap too quickly into broad and wide-open questions of interpretation before cultivating command of the details and specific ideas in the text. (Coleman and Pimentel, 2012, pp. 7–10)

☐ Lead (and have students lead) substantive discussions in which students have to respond to peers, paraphrase what was said, ask for clarification, and revise their own ideas if necessary. Make sure your discussions don't consist of just "teacher asks, student answers, teacher asks, student answers." But don't assume that students already know how to respond effectively to one another. Spend time explicitly teaching speaking and listening skills. See the following strategies.

Strategies for Teaching Speaking and Listening Skills

- Model speaking and listening. For example, show that when you listen, you might make eye contact or nod. You might also summarize what the person ahead of you said before jumping into your own point.

- Have students set goals before a discussion and assess themselves after. For example, goals might include "speak at least three times," "agree or disagree with someone else in detail," "ask a question," and "keep an open mind" (Roberts and Billings, 2012, p. 21).

- Keep a map of students' talk turns so you can identify patterns. Roberts and Billings suggest having students sit in a circle during a discussion. Draw the seating pattern on a piece of paper (draw a circle and write students' names around it to show where they're sitting). During the discussion, draw arrows on the circle and take notes to keep track of who is responding to whom. This will help you see which sets of friends respond only to one another, which students rarely participate, etc.

- Record class discussions, and show the DVD to students afterward. This will help them be aware of their own habits. For example, students who "hog" the conversation might not realize that they do so.

- Use a variety of group formats so students have practice speaking in small and large groups.

- Teach students to respond to the text during a discussion. You might wish to start with a short passage in which the lines are numbered. Require students to cite a line number and/or phrase as evidence when they respond. Eventually, students won't need as many supports and will be able to have high-level discussions on their own.

Lesson Plans at a Glance

Lesson Plan 23   You're in Charge! Leading a Group Discussion

Lesson Plan 24   'Dear Sir' or 'What's Up?' Language Depends on Audience
Handout—Know Your Audience

Lesson Plan 25   Teach, Don't Bore! Creating Engaging Presentations
Handout—PowerPoint/Prezi Activity Sheet

Lesson Plan 26   Take Command of Your Audience! Presenting Your Findings
Handout—Presentation Activity Sheet

Lesson Plan 27   Sources, Sources Everywhere:
Integrating Multiple Sources of Information
Handout—Different Forms of Media

Lesson Plan 28   Good Evening, My Fellow Citizens: Evaluating a Speaker
Handout—Evaluate a Speaker and His or Her Speech

You're in Charge!

Leading a Group Discussion

Grade Levels: 9–10; can be used in grades 11 and 12 as a review

Time Frame: Approximately two class periods

Overview: According to the Common Core State Standards, students should participate in a wide range of conversations—not only those that are teacher-led but also those that are led by the students themselves. In this lesson, students will learn how to lead a group discussion on a text. They will work together to explore a text's meaning and will also work on issues involving group dynamics.

Common Core State Standards

- 9–10: Speaking and Listening, Standard 1: Initiate and participate effectively in a range of collaborative discussions (one-on-one, in groups, and teacher-led) with diverse partners on *grades 9–10 topics, texts, and issues,* building on others' ideas and expressing their own clearly and persuasively.

  a. Come to discussions prepared, having read and researched material under study; explicitly draw on that preparation by referring to evidence from texts and other research on the topic or issue to stimulate a thoughtful, well-reasoned exchange of ideas.
  b. Work with peers to set rules for collegial discussions and decision making (e.g., informal consensus, taking votes on key issues, presentation of alternate views), clear goals and deadlines, and individual roles as needed.
  c. Propel conversations by posing and responding to questions that relate the current discussion to broader themes or larger ideas; actively incorporate others into the discussion; and clarify, verify, or challenge ideas and conclusions.
  d. Respond thoughtfully to diverse perspectives, summarize points of agreement and disagreement, and, when warranted, qualify or justify their own views and understanding and make new connections in light of the evidence and reasoning presented.

Objectives

- Students will prepare to lead discussions on an excerpt from a challenging text.

- Students will practice discussion skills, such as posing thoughtful questions to their peers, asking their peers for clarification, and keeping the flow of the conversation going.

Background Knowledge Required

No particular background knowledge is required for this lesson.

Materials Needed

- Copies of an excerpt from "Dream Analysis" in Carl Jung's *Modern Man in Search of a Soul*, which can be found on Google Books. (Recommended: A five-paragraph excerpt, starting with the paragraph that begins, "No amount of skepticism and critical reserve" through the paragraph that begins, "A fundamental mistake") This text is challenging yet covers a topic that teens are likely to find interesting (interpreting their dreams), so they may be engaged in tackling the difficult language. However, this text is only a recommendation; the lesson can be done with an excerpt from any sufficiently complex and engaging text.

Agenda

1. **Introduction**: Tell students that they each will take a turn leading a discussion on a text. Explain that this is a college skill—a professor doesn't always lead the discussion the way high school teachers often do; instead, college teachers expect students to work independently in seminars. Ask students to describe some qualities of a good discussion leader (e.g., asks thoughtful questions, waits for others to respond, acknowledges others' opinions, etc.).

2. **Prepare for the Discussion** (one class period): Organize students into groups of five, and give them the five-paragraph Carl Jung excerpt. Each person in the group will lead a discussion on one of the five paragraphs. Students should come to class the next day having read the entire text and with four questions about their paragraphs to ask the group when they lead the discussion. Tell students to design their questions to help other students understand the text. Questions should focus on analyzing specific word choices and language in the text; they should not be broad, opinion-based questions such as, "Do you agree with this message?" or "Did you like this paragraph?" Remind students that they don't have to know the answers to the questions they're posing. The point is to make meaning together as a group.

   In addition to preparing questions, students need to consider how they will facilitate the discussion. Go over some tips for being an effective discussion leader, such as

   - keeping the discussion on track if it goes off on a tangent
   - encouraging all students in the group to speak up
   - summarizing what someone says during the discussion and then asking other people to weigh in on it, rather than allowing people to make isolated comments in response to your question
   - asking students to verify or clarify their ideas, or challenging their ideas.

   The point is to get a smooth exchange of ideas going, not just to solicit answers.
   You can have students write down these tips and bring them to class as a little cheat sheet while they're leading the discussion, or you can have students create their own goals for being discussion leader (based on these things) and then assess themselves after the discussion to see how well they met their goals.

3. **During the Discussion** (next class period): Walk around and monitor each group, but try not to cut in; it's OK if students don't "get it right" the first time.

4. **After the Discussion**: Have students write paragraphs reflecting on how they did as discussion leaders and as participants when their classmates were leading. Students should reflect on their communication skills and think about how the format aided their understanding of the text.

Differentiation

For students who need extra support

- Model what you expect from a discussion leader.

- Help students with some of the challenging vocabulary in the text.

- Give group leaders some sentence starters, such as these:

  - Interesting idea—what was it about that word/sentence that made you feel that way? (to ask for verification)
  - I'm not sure I understood what you meant by X; can you give me a little more detail about it? (to ask for clarification)
  - That's an interesting point, but I wonder how to reconcile that with what the author says in the next sentence. (to challenge ideas)

For advanced students

- Have students practice acknowledging the previous person's comments, as this is an advanced skill that requires paraphrasing or summarizing. In other words, students don't just say, "Good point, Joe." They must summarize or paraphrase what the person said before asking for clarification or verification or before asking someone else to chime in.

Assessment

- Walk around and listen to group leaders pose questions on their paragraphs.

- Evaluate students' reflection paragraphs.

- You will continually assess this throughout the year as students gain more practice with discussions, and discussions become more complex.

Additional Resources

- Roberts, Terry, and Laura Billings. *Teaching Critical Thinking: Using Seminars for 21st Century Literacy*. Larchmont: Eye On Education, 2012. This book focuses on the Paideia Seminar but includes great ideas for getting students to hold balanced discussions.

Notes

After implementing the lesson, reflect on what worked and what you would change the next time.

_____

_____

_____

_____

'Dear Sir' or 'What's Up?'

Language Depends on Audience

Grade Levels: 9–10

Time Frame: Approximately two class periods

Overview: In this lesson, students will think critically about how language can and should be adjusted according to one's audience and purpose. This lesson should ideally be done toward the beginning of the year because it will help students with their upcoming speaking and writing projects.

Common Core State Standards

- 9–10: Speaking and Listening, Standard 1: Initiate and participate effectively in a range of collaborative discussions (one-on-one, in groups, and teacher-led) with diverse partners on *grades 9–10 topics, texts, and issues*, building on others' ideas and expressing their own clearly and persuasively.

- 9–10: Speaking and Listening, Standard 4: Present information, findings, and supporting evidence clearly, concisely, and logically such that listeners can follow the line of reasoning and the organization, development, substance, and style are appropriate to purpose, audience, and task.

Objectives

- Students will recognize their own language use for different situations in their personal lives and in school.

- Students will adapt their language according to audience and purpose.

Background Knowledge Required

No special background knowledge is necessary for this lesson.

Materials Needed

- Copies of the handout: Know Your Audience, p. 110

Agenda

1. **Introduction**: Ask students to name some of the different forms in which they communicate in and outside of school. (Possible answers: through texts, Tweets, Facebook, e-mails, in person, etc.) Ask: "How does your speaking and writing style vary for each format? Are you more careful about spelling, punctuation, and grammar with certain formats than with others?"

2. **Group Activity**: Tell students that no form of communication is right or wrong but depends on context—a form has to be appropriate for the audience and for the situation. Organize students into groups of three. Give each group the handout. For each situation on the handout, the group has to decide on the degree of formal language required. Groups should share their decisions with the full class. Note that not every group has to agree, but they have to justify their decisions.

3. **Independent Work**: Have students think about something that was in the news recently. It can be a sports, cultural, or political event. They should write about it three ways: as a 140-character tweet, as a 300-word post on a blog that is mostly read by their friends, and as a 500-word article for the local paper. Require accurate use of sources if applicable. Ask each student to share one of his or her three pieces with the full class.

4. **Wrap-Up** (next class period): Ask students to write short reflections about what they learned from the exercise and how that will apply to their speaking and writing throughout the year in your class.

Extend the Lesson

- This lesson will come in handy throughout the year as students complete a variety of oral presentations and writing assignments. Make sure to discuss your language expectations for each project you assign, and don't always make them the same. Students need to learn to adjust their speaking and writing styles for different contexts.

Differentiation

For students who need extra support

- Provide more examples of how language changes for different contexts before asking students to do the handout.

For advanced students

- Students who are familiar with concise Twitter writing can help other students who are not experienced at condensing information into 140 characters.

Assessment

- Evaluate whether students were able to justify their decisions during the handout activity.

- Evaluate students' writing for an awareness of how to change one's language based on audience.

- Read students' reflections to see if they are gaining an understanding of audience.

Additional Resources

- The following ReadWriteThink lesson explores appropriate language use: www.readwritethink.org/resources/resource-print.html?id=159.

Notes

After implementing the lesson, reflect on what worked and what you would change the next time.

_____

_____

_____

_____

Name: _____   Date: _____

Know Your Audience

Rank each situation on the scale from least formal to most formal language required. Put an X in the box.

1. Tweeting about a celebrity's performance at the Grammys

Least formal   Most formal

2. Talking to your teammates on the basketball court

Least formal   Most formal

3. Updating your Facebook status

Least formal   Most formal

4. Writing a thank-you note to a teacher who wrote you a college recommendation

Least formal   Most formal

5. Talking to your guidance counselor about scholarship applications

Least formal   Most formal

6. Writing a scientific report about the steps in a chemistry experiment

Least formal   Most formal

7. Writing an essay about the role of power in *Macbeth*

Least formal   Most formal

8. Delivering a speech to classmates persuading them to vote for you for student council

Least formal   Most formal

9. Going on a college interview

Least formal   Most formal

10. E-mailing a close friend about your post-prom ideas

Least formal   Most formal

Teach, Don't Bore!

Creating Engaging Presentations

Grade Levels: 9–10; can be adapted to grades 11–12 (see note in Overview)

Time Frame: Approximately four class periods.

Overview: The Common Core State Standards emphasize the importance of teaching students to use digital media effectively. In this lesson, students use digital media for an authentic purpose—to teach others about a current political issue in their school or community. To adapt this lesson for students in grades 11 and 12, make sure students include a "clear and distinct perspective" when they present their information. That phrase makes Standard 4 a higher level in grades 11–12 than in grades 9–10.

Common Core State Standards

- 9–10: Writing, Standard 2: Write informative/explanatory texts to examine and convey complex ideas, concepts, and information clearly and accurately through the effective selection, organization, and analysis of content.

- 9–10: Speaking and Listening, Standard 4: Present information, findings, and supporting evidence clearly, concisely, and logically such that listeners can follow the line of reasoning and the organization, development, substance, and style are appropriate to purpose, audience, and task.

- 9–10: Speaking and Listening, Standard 5: Make strategic use of digital media (e.g., textual, graphical, audio, visual, and interactive elements) in presentations to enhance understanding of findings, reasoning, and evidence and to add interest.

Objectives

- Students will research multiple sources to gather and select content.

- Students will consider the benefits of adding digital media to a presentation and what those visuals should include.

- Students will create PowerPoint or Prezi presentations using their research.

Background Knowledge Required

Students should have prior experience conducting research and integrating sources, as taught in the previous lesson.

Materials Needed

- Sample PowerPoint presentations: free ones on a variety of topics are available online.

- Computers with Internet connections for online research and PowerPoint or Prezi software

- Copies of the handout: PowerPoint/Prezi Activity Sheet, p. 116

Agenda

1. **Introduction**: Ask students if they think there are ways to get involved in the upcoming local and national elections, even if they are not old enough to vote. Collect their responses on the board. Explain the importance of being informed about the issues. Tell students that there are a lot of issues to learn about when making an informed decision about which candidates to support. Tell students that it might be hard for each student to research all the issues, so you'd like them to teach one another. Have each student choose a topic, such as health care, education, the environment, etc. and research where a political candidate stands on that issue, including his or her track record on that issue if applicable. Tell students that they will present their information during an Understand the Candidates event. If possible, you can broaden the audience and invite parents and other community members to attend. In that way, students will teach one another *and* adults outside of their circle. The wider audience may make students feel more excited to do a good job.

2. **Lesson 1** (approximately two class periods): Students should gather information on their topics and take notes that they will turn into presentations. As a full class, brainstorm a list of reliable types of sources for different types of information (e.g., a candidate's website, news articles about the candidate, etc.). Tell students to consult at least three different sources of information. Consulting multiple sources will help them find the clearest, most relevant information. It will also help students spot weak or erroneous sources. Don't forget to remind students about bias—students should be on the lookout for sites created by the opposition that do not show a candidate's true beliefs on a topic.

3. **Lesson 2** (one class period): Ask students how multimedia and visuals can help people understand and remember information. Write students' responses on the board. Tell students that they will be required to present their findings using Power-Point (or Prezi) software with multimedia (video clips, audio clips, images, etc.). Mention the importance of using visuals that evoke comparisons or create metaphor as opposed to reading word for word from the screen. Show students examples of successful and unsuccessful PowerPoints. Don't tell them which ones are good and which ones are bad; have students decide for themselves and explain their opinions. Then, as a class, decide on five qualities of an effective PowerPoint (or Prezi) presentation. Tell students they will have to incorporate those qualities into their presentations. Require about seven to ten slides. Remind students to consider their audience—intelligent young people but perhaps with little or no background knowledge about some of these political issues (and maybe adults who are making voting decisions, if you extend the audience). What needs to be defined, simplified, or clarified for this audience?

4. **Independent Work** (in class and for homework): Have students review the information they gathered and decide how to express it using PowerPoint (or Prezi). Students should choose key details about their politicians' stances to list on the slides. They should also incorporate a few multimedia components that help people understand

the issue. Have students workshop their slide drafts with partners; they can help remove unnecessary information or add missing information to the slides. Remind students to add notes about what they might say as they're showing the slides. You should also walk around and provide feedback before students complete their final versions.

Extend the Lesson

- Pass out copies of the handout, and organize students into small groups. Each group should discuss the sample PowerPoints and their class notes to determine the qualities of an effective presentation. Students should fill in the handout to show how they think the slides in their presentations should be evaluated. Remind them that at this point, the slides themselves, not an oral presentation of the slides, will be evaluated. Have each group share its completed rubric with the full class.

Differentiation

For students who need extra support

- Provide more one-on-one support as they prepare their slides.

- Provide specific suggestions, either to individual students or via a list on the board, about what kinds of multimedia to consider.

- Encourage students to review the examples of successful PowerPoint presentations after they complete the drafts of their own, looking for ways to improve their drafts.

For advanced students

- Ask volunteers to explain to the full class which parts of their presentations they are most confident about.

- Ask questions and allow other students to ask questions, managing the discussion so that advanced students act as mentors to students who need extra support.

Assessment

- Check students' understanding of the reasons to add multimedia to their presentations. Ask students to revise slides that are packed with too much visual information or too much text.

- Evaluate the handouts to see that students included key elements of an effective presentation in the top-score box, with the bullets in lower boxes showing a decrease in achievement of the key elements.

- Use the student-created rubrics or the following rubric to evaluate students' final drafts of their slides.

Score 4.0	The student • Uses seven to ten slides to explain a candidate's position on an issue. • Includes relevant multimedia that makes the issue clear. • Includes words, phrases, or short sentences to help make the issue clear, as needed. Text is clear and concise. No major errors or omissions in the score 4.0 content.

Score 3.5	The student demonstrates success at the 3.0 level plus partial success at the 4.0 level.
Score 3.0	The student • Uses five or fewer slides to explain a candidate's position on an issue. • Includes relevant multimedia to help explain the procedure, though the multimedia components may be used too sparingly or be overdone. • Includes words, phrases, or short sentences to help make the issue clear, as needed. Text may need editing for clarity or conciseness. No major errors or omissions in the score 3.0 content.
Score 2.5	The student demonstrates success at the 2.0 level plus partial success at the 3.0 level.
Score 2.0	The student • Uses three or fewer slides to explain a candidate's position on an issue. • Includes multimedia components, though some are irrelevant, unclear, and/or overdone. • Includes words, phrases, or short sentences, though text is unclear and/or overused. No major errors or omissions in the score 2.0 content.
Score 1.5	The student demonstrates partial success at the 2.0 level.
Score 1.0	With help, the student achieves partial success at score 2.0 and 3.0 contents.
Score 0.5	With help, the student achieves partial success at score 2.0 content but not score 3.0 content.
Score 0.0	Even with help, the student has no success.

Additional Resources

- Prezi can be found at prezi.com.

- Consult Mike Splane's "PowerPoint Presentation Advice" for additional tips to share with your students: www.cob.sjsu.edu/splane_m/PresentationTips.htm.

Notes

After implementing the lesson, reflect on what worked and what you would change the next time.

_____

_____

_____

_____

PowerPoint/Prezi Activity Sheet

Complete the rubric below by filling in bullet items to show what makes an effective PowerPoint or Prezi presentation. A top-score presentation should effectively use the most important elements, or parts, of a PowerPoint or Prezi presentation. Lower scores indicate that important parts may be missing or have errors.

Score 4.0	The student • • • No major errors or omissions in the score 4.0 content.
Score 3.5	The student demonstrates success at the 3.0 level plus partial success at the 4.0 level.
Score 3.0	The student • • • No major errors or omissions in the score 3.0 content.
Score 2.5	The student demonstrates success at the 2.0 level plus partial success at the 3.0 level.
Score 2.0	The student • • • No major errors or omissions in the score 2.0 content.
Score 1.5	The student demonstrates partial success at the 2.0 level.
Score 1.0	With help, the student achieves partial success at score 2.0 and 3.0 contents.
Score 0.5	With help, the student achieves partial success at score 2.0 content but not score 3.0 content.
Score 0.0	Even with help, the student has no success.

Take Command of Your Audience!

Presenting Your Findings

Grade Levels: 9–10; can also be done in grades 11–12 (see note in Overview)

Time Frame: Approximately two or three class periods

Overview: Students will learn speaking skills required when delivering a formal presentation. This lesson immediately follows Lesson Plan 25 on page 112. This lesson can be repeated in each grade level in high school. It takes a while for some people (including adults) to feel comfortable speaking in front of an audience, and the more practice, the better.

Common Core State Standards
- 9–10: Speaking and Listening, Standard 4: Present information, findings, and supporting evidence clearly, concisely, and logically such that listeners can follow the line of reasoning and the organization, development, substance, and style are appropriate to purpose, audience, and task.

- 9–10: Speaking and Listening, Standard 6: Adapt speech to a variety of contexts and tasks, demonstrating command of formal English when indicated or appropriate.

Objectives
- Students will deliver a PowerPoint or Prezi presentation.

- Students will practice using eye contact, adequate speaking volume, and clear pronunciation during an oral presentation.

- Students will give one another collegial feedback on their presentations.

Background Knowledge Required
Use this lesson after students create presentations on an assigned or a selected topic, such as the presentation created in Lesson Plan 25.

Materials Needed
- Students' PowerPoint or Prezi presentations

- Computers with PowerPoint or Prezi software

- Copies of the handout: Presentation Activity Sheet, p. 121

Agenda

1. **Introduction**: Tell students that they have worked really hard on creating engaging presentations, but engaging presentations need engaging presenters! Ask: "What are the qualities of a good presenter?" Write responses on the board. They might include the following:

   - Don't just read the slides aloud; summarize the information.
   - Look at the audience.
   - Speak loudly and clearly, etc.

2. **Teacher Modeling**: Read a short speech in a couple of different styles: without a lot of eye contact, too fast or too slowly, etc. Have students comment on what is effective and what you could improve. Use this discussion as an opportunity to give students tips on how to give respectful, effective feedback. For example, comments (even given jokingly) such as "That's so lame!" or "You sound like a mouse" are not helpful. Comments such as "You started out speaking clearly, but then you started saying your words too fast" are more helpful. Remind students that public speaking can be nerve-racking, even for professionals, and that a supportive audience and peers who want to help someone improve can make all the difference.

3. **Partner Work**: Organize students into pairs, distribute the handouts, and have students work with their partners to complete the handout (rubric for evaluating presentations).

4. **Practice**: Have students practice saying their presentations to their partners. If time permits, have each student work with two different partners (one at a time) so that students can get two different perspectives. You could also have students record their partners' presentations so that students can listen to and watch themselves and see what they would like to improve. Students often aren't aware of their own habits unless they get a chance to see and hear them.

5. **Wrap-Up**: When students finish practicing, have them deliver their presentations to their real audience! That audience might be a group of their peers, or it might be a wider audience that includes parents, school leaders, and community members.

Extend the Lesson

- Have students post their slides or recordings of their live presentations on a classroom website, a personal website, or a public website such as YouTube. (Note that you may need school and parent approval.)

Differentiation

For students who need extra support

- Allow students more time to prepare their presentations. Help them one-on-one with any pronunciation issues or other concerns.

For advanced students

- Have those students take on extra speaking roles. For example, they can emcee during the live presentations by introducing their classmates' presentations.

- Ask technologically skilled students to stand by on presentation day to help trouble-shoot the presentation software for their peers. Have one student on standby during each presentation, watching for signs of trouble. If a presenter is timid, ask a confident troubleshooter to stand just behind and to the side of the presenter so the timid person doesn't feel so alone in front of the audience.

Assessment

- Monitor students during the practice activity, listening for acceptable and unacceptable feedback. Take a break midway through the work period to give students examples of some of the respectful and disrespectful comments you heard.

- Evaluate students' work on the handout to see that they included key elements of an effective presentation in the top-score box, with the bullets in lower boxes showing a decrease in achievement of the key elements.

- After the live presentations, ask students to write paragraphs evaluating their performances, noting strengths and what they would change next time.

- Use a student-created rubric or the following rubric to evaluate students' live presentations.

- When it is not a student's turn to present, he or she should actively listen to the person presenting, write down one thing he or she learned from the presentation, and turn it in to you. In that way, students will be listening to one another and not just waiting for their turns. This also allows you to assess listening skills in addition to speaking skills.

Score 4.0	The student • Speaks in a natural, unhurried voice. • Speaks loudly enough to be heard clearly in the back row. • Makes eye contact with each section of the audience (left, right, front, back). • Uses techniques such as repetition of key points and humor to engage the audience. • Answers questions clearly and concisely. No major errors or omissions in the score 4.0 content.
Score 3.5	The student demonstrates success at the 3.0 level plus partial success at the 4.0 level.
Score 3.0	The student • Speaks most of the time in a natural, unhurried voice. • Speaks most of the time in a clearly audible voice. • Makes some eye contact with the audience. • Attempts to engage the audience once or twice by repeating a key point or using humor (even if the audience doesn't laugh!). • Answers questions, though answers might be too brief or may ramble. No major errors or omissions in the score 3.0 content.

Score 2.5	The student demonstrates success at the 2.0 level plus partial success at the 3.0 level.
Score 2.0	The student • Speaks too quickly most of the time. • Speaks too loudly or too quietly most of the time. • Makes eye contact with the audience once or twice. • Answers questions, though answers might be too brief or may ramble. No major errors or omissions in the score 2.0 content.
Score 1.5	The student demonstrates partial success at the 2.0 level.
Score 1.0	With help, the student achieves partial success at score 2.0 and 3.0 contents.
Score 0.5	With help, the student achieves partial success at score 2.0 content but not score 3.0 content.
Score 0.0	Even with help, the student has no success.

Additional Resources

- This site has a good list of tips for effectively delivering a presentation: go.owu.edu/ ~dapeople/ggpresnt.html.

Notes

After implementing the lesson, reflect on what worked and what you would change the next time.

_____

_____

_____

_____

Name: _____ Date: _____

Presentation Activity Sheet

Complete the rubric below by filling in bullet items to show what makes an effective oral presentation. A top-score presentation should demonstrate key speaking skills. Lower scores indicate that key skills were used only partly successfully or left out.

Score 4.0	The student ▪ ▪ ▪ No major errors or omissions in the score 4.0 content.
Score 3.5	The student demonstrates success at the 3.0 level plus partial success at the 4.0 level.
Score 3.0	The student ▪ ▪ ▪ No major errors or omissions in the score 3.0 content.
Score 2.5	The student demonstrates success at the 2.0 level plus partial success at the 3.0 level.
Score 2.0	The student ▪ ▪ ▪ No major errors or omissions in the score 2.0 content.
Score 1.5	The student demonstrates partial success at the 2.0 level.
Score 1.0	With help, the student achieves partial success at score 2.0 and 3.0 contents.
Score 0.5	With help, the student achieves partial success at score 2.0 content but not score 3.0 content.
Score 0.0	Even with help, the student has no success.

Sources, Sources Everywhere

Integrating Multiple Sources of Information

Grade Levels: 9–12

Time Frame: Approximately one or two class periods

Overview: In this lesson, students practice thinking critically about how (and why) information is presented in different media formats. Students are asked to integrate information from some of these formats to make informed decisions. Hybrid cars are the topic here, but you can use this lesson with any topic of your choosing.

Common Core State Standards

- 9–10: Speaking and Listening, Standard 2: Integrate multiple sources of information presented in diverse media or formats (e.g., visually, quantitatively, orally) evaluating the credibility and accuracy of each source.

- 11–12: Speaking and Listening, Standard 2: Integrate multiple sources of information presented in diverse formats or media (e.g., visually, quantitatively, orally) in order to make informed decisions and solve problems, evaluating the credibility and accuracy of each source and noting any discrepancies among the data.

Objectives

- Students will consider the benefits and drawbacks of different media formats, such as videos, blogs, tweets, ads, newspaper articles, and magazine articles.

- Students will synthesize information from various sources to make informed decisions.

Background Knowledge Required

No particular background knowledge is required for this lesson.

Materials Needed

- Copies of the handout: Different Forms of Media, p. 125. The handout uses a table format. You can also use a matrix graphic organizer to help students see points of comparison among various sources.

- Internet access

Agenda

1. **Introduction**: Ask students how they gather information when making decisions about products they want, whether they buy them themselves or ask their parents for them. "Do you read reviews, watch videos, look at ads, or listen to commercials?" If they consult more than one source, how do they compare and integrate the information to make informed choices? How does the amount of research change depending on the importance of the decision? If they haven't done this kind of research before, how *would* they do it if asked to make decisions on their own?

2. **Mini-Lesson**: Ask students to imagine that they are ready to buy a car and are debating whether to get a hybrid. On the one hand, they want to help the environment; on the other hand, they're not sure hybrids are the answer. How would they go about making a decision? Have the class brainstorm at least five *types* of sources they would consult (e.g., an ad or website for a particular hybrid model, a blog post written by a car enthusiast about hybrids, a print or online article about hybrids, a *Consumer Reports* article rating hybrid models, a TV news segment about the growing popularity of hybrid cars, a how-to video showing how hybrids work, etc.). Have students come up with the negatives and positives of each type of source (including which type might be more biased, which would include more thorough information, etc.). Complete part 1 of the handout as a full class. (Note: To make this easier, you can say that price is not an option and have students focus only on convenience, safety, and effect on the environment.)

3. **Group Work**: Organize students into groups of three or four. Have each group conduct research and gather information on hybrids from a variety of sources (at least five specific sources representing one of each of the types they brainstormed in the mini-lesson). Ask students to complete part 2 of the handout.

4. **Wrap-Up** (may extend to the next class period): Ask students to decide whether a hybrid would be a worthwhile investment for someone about to buy a car. Students should write paragraphs summarizing their research and their decisions. They should write additional paragraphs reflecting on what they learned about the benefits and drawbacks of different forms of media sources.

Extend the Lesson

- Put students on the other side of the picture. Have students imagine that they work for a hybrid company. Ask them what forms of media they would use to disseminate information about their product. Why?

Differentiation

For students who need extra support

- Organize students into groups based on skill level so that you can spend more time with certain groups.

For advanced students

- Organize the groups so that struggling students are paired with more advanced students who can assist them.

Assessment

- Evaluate students' handouts, paragraphs, and reflections to see whether they thought critically about the different kinds of mediums and how they help people make informed decisions.

Additional Resources

- This chart lists different mediums and their benefits and drawbacks: 63.175.159.26/~cimh/cami/files/PUBCOMM/PresK11/PDF/Media%20Matrix.2.pdf. Have students pretend that they work for a company that sells a certain type of service or that promotes a cause. Ask them which media format they would use to spread the news about that service or cause.

Notes

After implementing the lesson, reflect on what worked and what you would change the next time.

_____

_____

_____

_____

Name: _____   Date: _____

Different Forms of Media

Part 1: Make a list of different types of media that might provide information on hybrid cars (e.g., ads, websites, etc.). What are the benefits and drawbacks of each?

Medium	Benefits	Drawbacks

Part 2: Find actual sources on hybrid cars and evaluate them. Make notes in the table. Then answer the questions that follow.

Source	Information provided	Information excluded
Source 1		
Source 2		
Source 3		
Source 4		
Source 5		

Where did the sources agree?

_____

_____

Where did the sources disagree? Did you find any discrepancies among the data provided about hybrid cars?

_____

_____

Good Evening, My Fellow Citizens

Evaluating a Speaker

Grade Levels: 9–12

Time Frame: Approximately two class periods

Overview: This lesson guides students through the process of analyzing delivery techniques and rhetorical techniques in a speech by President John F. Kennedy.

Common Core State Standards

- 9–10: Speaking and Listening, Standard 3: Evaluate a speaker's point of view, reasoning, and use of evidence and rhetoric, identifying any fallacious reasoning or exaggerated or distorted evidence.

- 11–12: Speaking and Listening, Standard 3: Evaluate a speaker's point of view, reasoning, and use of evidence and rhetoric, assessing the stance, premises, links among ideas, word choice, points of emphasis, and tone used.

- 9–10: Reading, Informational Text, Standard 8: Delineate and evaluate the argument and specific claims in a text, assessing whether the reasoning is valid and the evidence is relevant and sufficient; identify false statements and fallacious reasoning.

- 11–12: Reading, Informational Text, Standard 8: Delineate and evaluate the reasoning in seminal U.S. texts, including the application of constitutional principles and use of legal reasoning . . . and the premises, purposes, and arguments in works of public advocacy (e.g., *The Federalist*, presidential addresses).

- 9–10: Reading, Informational Text, Standard 9: Analyze seminal U.S. documents of historical and literary significance (e.g., Washington's "Farewell Address," the "Gettysburg Address," Roosevelt's "Four Freedoms" speech, King's "Letter from Birmingham Jail"), including how they address related themes and concepts.

- 11–12: Reading, Informational Text, Standard 9: Analyze seventeenth-, eighteenth-, and nineteenth-century foundational U.S. documents of historical and literary significance (including the Declaration of Independence, the Preamble to the Constitution, the Bill of Rights, and Lincoln's "Second Inaugural Address") for their themes, purposes, and rhetorical features.

Objectives

- Students will listen to an excerpt of a seminal U.S. speech of historical and literary significance and practice their listening comprehension skills.
- Students will analyze a speaker's rhetoric.

Background Knowledge Required

Students should be familiar with the terms *audience, tone,* and *point of view*.

Materials Needed

- Partial video recording and partial transcript of President Kennedy's speech "Report to the American People on Civil Rights," delivered June 11, 1963. You can find a video and a transcript of the speech on the website of the John F. Kennedy Presidential Library and Museum: www.jfklibrary.org/Asset-Viewer/LH8F_0Mzv0e6Ro1yEm74Ng .aspx. For this lesson, plan to use the first five minutes and 41 seconds of the video. That segment corresponds to the first 12 paragraphs of the transcript.
- A computer with Internet access, speakers, and a monitor to show the text of the speech to the class.
- Copies of the handout: Evaluate a Speaker and His or Her Speech, p. 132

Agenda

1. **Introduction**: Begin class with a five-minute writing task that focuses students' attention on the topic of a live speech and its ability to influence an audience. Here is a suggested task:

   > Think of a time when a speech, either formal or informal, influenced you to take an action or adopt a point of view. What do you remember about the speech? What do you remember about how it influenced you?

   It isn't necessary to share students' responses with the full group. However, if you think doing so will further engage students' interest and willingness to open up and participate during the rest of the class, then you may want to take the time for full-class sharing.

2. **Background Information**: Pass out copies of the handout, and have students fill in part 1 as you introduce the speech and give background information on it.

   a. Name of speaker: President John F. Kennedy
   b. Title of speech: "Report to the American People on Civil Rights, 11 June 1963" Remind students that they should enclose the title of a speech in quotation marks.
   c. Date of delivery: June 11, 1963
   d. Occasion of the speech (historical context): "In his speech, the President responds to the threats of violence and obstruction on the University of Alabama campus following desegregation attempts" (quote from the "About Video" section of the web page).
   e. Intended audience: All Americans, but especially whites, and Congress

3. **Listen to the Speech**: Ask students to look at part 2 of the handout, items 6 and 7. As they watch and listen to the speech excerpt, they can use the graphic organizer to record specific details and ideas about the speaker's tone and facial expressions. Next, play the speech. Finally, give students a few additional minutes to add more details to items 6 and 7 and to write a response to item 8. Here are some possible responses:

   f. Measured, serious, carefully paced, reasonable, a pause after each phrase or word group in sentence, conversational volume of voice with no spikes up or down, not very emotional

   g. Solemn, serious, regular eye contact broken by moments of glancing at notes, no smiles or other variations on the rather flat facial expression.

   h. The topic of the speech involves civil unrest, which is a volatile topic. However, the solemn, measured, and nearly emotionless delivery influenced me to look at the facts and not get emotional about the topic. I didn't feel provoked to argue with the speaker but rather to consider his points with respect and with the same seriousness he treated them with.

4. **Full-Class Sharing**: As a class, go over possible responses on part 2 of the handout.

5. **Read the Transcript**: Pass out copies of the speech excerpt. Ask students to follow along on their transcripts as they listen again.

6. **Mini-Lesson on Rhetoric**: Explain that *rhetoric* is the art of effective or persuasive speaking or writing. Examples of *rhetorical techniques* include these, among others:

   ▪ Repetition of words and phrases to create rhythm, impact, and memorability
   ▪ Rhetorical questions to engage the audience's active involvement in processing the speaker's (or writer's) ideas
   ▪ Pacing of information. How rapidly or slowly does the speaker reveal main points? Are ideas packaged in long, complex sentences and paragraphs? Or shorter, more accessible sentences and paragraphs?
   ▪ Allusions to revered documents or people, aka "appeal to authority"
   ▪ The use of hard data, aka "appeal to logic"
   ▪ The use of emotionally charged words and phrases. You can link this topic to a review of words' denotations vs. connotations.

7. **Small-Group Activity**: Organize students into pairs or small groups and ask them to complete part 3 of the handout. Here are suggested answers:

   i. Racial integration of American society, overdue by 100 years. Paragraphs 2, 3, and 12 provide related evidence. Also see the "heart of the question" sentence that begins paragraph 11.

   j. Racial integration and the protection of civil rights for all is the morally correct path for the nation. Note that students need to infer the speaker's point of view on the main topic. For evidence, look at how the speaker begins the first sentence of paragraphs 4, 5, 6, and 7—"I hope," "we are committed," "It ought to be possible," and "It ought to be possible"—and then look at the details that follow each point of argument.

k. Paragraphs 4–12 all offer one or more reasons to support the speaker's point of view. Students might paraphrase or quote strong ideas or summarize paragraphs.

l. Rhetorical techniques include but aren't limited to

- repetition ("It ought to be possible" in paragraphs 5, 6, and 7; the word *issue* in paragraphs 9 and 10; "If he cannot" in paragraph 11; "They are not yet freed" in paragraph 12)
- rhetorical questions (paragraph 11)
- pacing (short paragraphs)
- allusions to revered documents (paragraph 10)
- the use of hard data (paragraph 8)
- the use of emotionally charged words and phrases—*threats* and *defiant statements* in paragraph 2, *peacefully* and *constructive* in paragraph 3, *rights* and *free* in paragraph 11; and other words (Note that this part of the lesson may continue into the next class period.)

8. **Full-Class Sharing**: Have groups share their responses on part 3 of the handout, making sure that exemplar responses are identified for each numbered item.

9. **Wrap-Up**: Have students complete a five-minute writing task in response to this question: What does the oral delivery of the speech segment accomplish that the written transcript does not?

Extend the Lesson

- Have students deliver favorite paragraphs from the speech, using their own choices of tone and delivery techniques. Have students explain why they did or didn't vary from JFK's delivery techniques. (Speaking and Listening Standard 4)

- Link the lesson to a mini-research lesson by having students find the texts of President Lincoln's Emancipation Proclamation, the Civil Rights Act of 1866, the Civil Rights Act of 1964, and information about the desegregation of education (e.g., the story of Ruby Bridges). (Writing Standards 7 and 8)

- Further extend the lesson to include conversations via technology by having students create blog entries on their research findings, including making comments on others' blogs and replying to comments on their own blogs. (Writing Standard 6)

Differentiation

For students who need extra support

- Encourage multiple encounters with the speech and the transcript by providing the URL of the video, in addition to the transcript. If the language of the speech is especially challenging to students, add an activity that asks students to use context clues, dictionaries, and other techniques to determine word meanings, and then have students share their work.

For advanced students

- Allow the option of working independently to complete part 3 of the handout.

Assessment

- Have students write a reflective piece on the topic "What I learned about public speaking from President John F. Kennedy." There is a checklist of strong and weak elements of reflective writing in the assessment section of Lesson Plan 22 (see page 96). Alternatively, ask each student to voice aloud one reflective point in response to the prompt.

Additional Resources

- To find other seminal U.S. speeches to use to repeat or adapt this lesson, consider the texts, and often audio recordings, of the 100 American speeches archived on American Rhetoric: www.americanrhetoric.com/top100speechesall.html.

Notes

After implementing the lesson, reflect on what worked and what you would change the next time.

_____

_____

_____

_____

Evaluate a Speaker and His or Her Speech

Use the recorded speech excerpt and transcript provided by your teacher to jot down details, examples, ideas, direct quotations, and other evidence for each category below.

Part 1: Background Information

1. Name of speaker: _____

2. Title of speech: _____

3. Date of delivery: _____

4. Occasion of the speech (historical context): _____

    _____

5. Intended audience: _____

Part 2: Listen to the Speech

6. Describe the speaker's tone of voice:	7. Describe the speaker's use of facial expressions and eye contact:

8. Tell how the speaker's use of audible and visual techniques (see your notes above) influenced your understanding of the speech:

Question	Evidence from Text to Support Answer
9. What is the main topic of the speech?	
10. What is the speaker's point of view on the main topic?	
11. What reasons did the speaker use to support his point of view? Choose four reasons that you think are especially strong. ■ ■ ■ ■	
12. Identify two rhetorical techniques the speaker used to make the speech effective or persuasive. ■ ■	

Language

Part 4

Overview

The Common Core State Standards for language cover the full range of conventions in grammar, usage, capitalization, punctuation, and spelling. However, they don't advocate teaching the rules in isolation; they require teaching students how the rules *apply* to language, style, and meaning. They also emphasize the importance of teaching students to adjust their language based on audience and purpose. Students don't always have to write in a formal style "for the teacher"; they can also write in informal styles, but they should learn to decide *when* a particular style is most appropriate.

In addition to emphasizing grammar and style, the standards also stress vocabulary. Teach words explicitly and also implicitly through your own word choices. Don't require students to memorize words and use them in sentences; help students truly understand what the words mean by using them in different contexts and analyzing shades of meaning. Focus on academic vocabulary, which is essential to students' success in school and beyond. Give students tools to uncover word meanings on their own so they can become more independent readers and writers. Following is a list of other key points to keep in mind when designing language lessons.

Planning Checklist

When planning a CCSS-based language lesson, keep the following tips in mind:

☐ Teach students grammar and conventions, and make sure that each year builds on the previous year. Students need to gain "mastery of the full range of grammar and conventions as they are applied in increasingly sophisticated contexts" (Coleman and Pimentel, 2012, p. 13).

☐ Help students understand language "as a matter of craft" and learn when it is necessary to use standard written and spoken English. Students need to learn to make effective language choices on their own, based on their audience and purpose.

☐ Give English language learners extra support (as necessary) with academic language. ELLs often pick up social language quickly but have a more difficult time with Tier Two academic words.

☐ Show students how to think critically about words when writing or analyzing an author's choices. Students should consider nuances in word meanings, figurative language, and connotations of words.

☐ Teach academic vocabulary (Tier Two) words implicitly and explicitly. Also teach domain-specific (Tier Three) words. Following are some strategies for teaching vocabulary.

Strategies for Teaching Vocabulary

▪ Teach context clues and when not to use them. Sometimes, it is necessary to consult a reference source to confirm a guess or find a meaning.

▪ Teach Greek and Latin affixes. This will help students expand their word knowledge and determine the meanings of unknown words.

▪ Don't have students memorize word lists and use them in sentences. Students will learn the words for a quiz and forget them days later. Have students explore the words in more depth, such as by relating the words to their own contexts and to other words they know. Benjamin and Crow (2013) provide the following example of how to engage students in vocabulary instruction:

> An example of a meaningful engagement would be for students to create a blog about a topic of interest and carry on an online conversation that is laced with target words. Even if the target words do sound forced, at least the students are combing through the new vocabulary in search of words that actually communicate their ideas. (p. 129)

▪ Choose relevant, academic vocabulary words to teach rather than the esoteric words of a novel. Averil Coxhead's Academic Word List can be found here: www.victoria.ac.nz/lals/resources/academicwordlist.

Lesson Plans at a Glance

Lesson Plan 29   Are They Really Synonyms? Understanding
Shades of Meaning in Words

Lesson Plan 30   Get Your Ducks in a Row: Creating Parallel Structure
Handout—Identify Parallel Structure

Lesson Plan 31   Everything in Its Place: MLA Style

Lesson Plan 32   If You Don't Get This Lesson, Explain It
to Me: Understanding Paradox

Lesson Plan 33   Are Those Words Working Together? Using Hyphens Correctly

Lesson Plan 34   Know When to Break the Rules:
Issues of Complex or Contested Usage
Handout—Decipher Complex Conventions of Grammar Usage

Lesson Plan 35   Notice Me! Notice Me! Vary Syntax for Effect
Handout—Analyze Syntax in Complex Texts

Are They Really Synonyms?

Understanding Shades of Meaning in Words

Grade Levels: 9–10

Time Frame: Approximately one class period

Overview: In this lesson, students learn about shades of meaning in words. Understanding nuances in word meanings will improve students' comprehension and help them make good decisions when writing.

Common Core State Standards

- 9–10: Language, Standard 5: Demonstrate understanding of figurative language, word relationships, and nuances in word meanings. b. Analyze nuances in the meanings of words with similar denotations.

- 9–10: Writing, Standard 5: Develop and strengthen writing as needed by planning, revising, editing, rewriting, or trying a new approach, focusing on addressing what is most significant for a specific purpose and audience.

Objectives

- Students will learn about shades of meaning and connotation.

- Students will consider word connotations while reading and writing.

Background Knowledge Required

No particular prior knowledge is necessary for this lesson.

Materials Needed:

- Students should come to class with drafts of an essay they are writing. Remind them the day before to bring them in.

Agenda

1. **Introduction**: Write a word on the board. Have students come up to the board and list some synonyms for that word. For example, if you write *confused*, they might add *bewildered*, *perplexed*, *baffled*, and *vexed*. Ask students if those words are true synonyms or if each one has a slightly different shade of meaning. Try each word in the same sample sentence and see how it affects the sentence's tone. Example: I'm really *confused* by the homework assignment vs. I'm really *bewildered* by the homework assignment. Which one carries more emotion and distress?

2. **Mini-Lesson**: Point out that words have different shades of meaning and slightly different tones (informal or more formal, etc.) and that writers must think critically about what words they select when they write or think about what authors might mean in their texts. Tell students that words can have a positive or a negative meaning. Give students a short excerpt to read independently or with a partner, and have them focus on word choice. They should pick five words from the text to analyze. Why did the author choose those exact words? How would a different synonym affect the meaning of that sentence or paragraph?

3. **Independent Work**: Have students go back to their own essays and look at their word choices. Do their words carry enough weight? Are they precise enough? Are there cases where different words would be better?

4. **Wrap-Up**: Have students share some of the word choice revisions they made.

Differentiation

For students who need extra support
- Have students practice this activity with easy words before they examine words in a text and before they examine the words in their own writing.

For advanced students
- Have students look at shades of meaning in advanced vocabulary words.

Assessment
- Check students' drafts to see whether they attempted to revise their word choices. Include word choice on the rubric you use to evaluate their essays.

Additional Resources
- This fun lesson teaches shades of meaning by having students analyze ways advertisers use certain words over others to convince people of something: www.visualthesaurus.com/cm/lessons/shades-of-meaning.

Notes
After implementing the lesson, reflect on what worked and what you would change the next time.

_____

_____

_____

_____

Get Your Ducks in a Row

Creating Parallel Structure

Grade Levels: 9–10

Time Frame: Approximately one or two class periods

Overview: This lesson introduces students to parallel structure in sentences. The phrase itself—*parallel structure*—can be intimidating, so the lesson begins with a non-threatening introduction of the term, building up to its use in grammar and sentence structure. The Common Core State Standards first require students to attend to parallel structure in grade 9, and they are expected to review and practice this aspect of usage through the rest of high school.

Common Core State Standards

- 9–10: Language, Standard 1: Demonstrate command of the conventions of standard English grammar and usage when writing or speaking. a. Use parallel structure.

- 9–10: Language, Standard 6: Acquire and use accurately general academic and domain-specific words and phrases, sufficient for reading, writing, speaking, and listening at the college and career-readiness levels; demonstrate independence in gathering vocabulary knowledge when considering a word or phrase important to comprehension or expression.

- 9–10: Writing, Standard 5: Develop and strengthen writing as needed by planning, revising, editing, rewriting, or trying a new approach, focusing on addressing what is most significant for a specific purpose and audience.

- 9–10: Speaking and Listening, Standard 1: Initiate and participate effectively in a range of collaborative discussions . . . with diverse partners on *grades 9-10 topics, texts, and issues,* building on others' ideas and expressing their own clearly and persuasively.

Objectives

- Students will identify parallel structure in others' writing.

- Students will use parallel structure in their own writing.

Background Knowledge Required

Students should know what phrases and clauses are.

Materials Needed

- For the homework activity, students should use drafts in progress or previously completed pieces of writing.

- Copies of the handout: Identify Parallel Structure, p. 144

Agenda

1. **Introduction**: Introduce the word *parallel*. Begin with a three-minute writing task on the following topic:

   > Tell me about something in your life, or something that you know about, that is parallel. Examples are the parallel bars in gymnastics, parallel fence posts, or parallel lanes on the highway.

   Read the writing task aloud, and make sure that students understand that *parallel* means "extending in the same direction and never crossing." Write the word, or the entire writing task, on the board so that students can see the word's spelling.

2. **Build Knowledge**: Ask a few volunteers to read their written pieces aloud. Make sure everyone clearly understands the basic meaning of *parallel*. To engage students' interest, ask volunteers to draw visuals on the board (parallel bars, parallel fence posts, parallel daisies—anything to show the concept). Build on this basic knowledge by telling students that *parallel* also means "similar." Ask students to offer examples of how two schools might have parallel codes of behavior, how two countries might have parallel points of economic interest, how two friends might have parallel athletic goals, and so on.

3. **Grammar Mini-Lesson**: Point to the visuals on the board (parallel fence posts, etc.), and think aloud about the neatness, order, and balance that parallel structure provides. To show a contrast, draw a crosshatch of falling fence posts, tangled daisy stems, or whatever. Think aloud about how this structure is more confusing and disorderly. Then explain that writers can use the concept of parallel structure to make sentences neat, orderly, and balanced. The result is a pleasing rhythm and flow in the writing.

   Write three categories on the board: words, phrases, clauses. Under each heading, write examples of parallel elements, explaining what makes them parallel. For instance, tell students to consider words. They can achieve parallel structure for words in lists by choosing all nouns, all verbs, all adjectives, and so on. The words' part of speech is parallel, or the same. Example: "My best friend is loyal, kind, and impulsive." That sentence has parallel structure. This one does not: "My best friend is loyal, shows kindness, and often impulsive." In the second sentence, the series of items is an adjective, a verb phrase, and an adverb-plus-adjective.

   Phrases work the same way. To be parallel, the phrases must have the same structure. Example: "Ralph loves playing football, sketching portraits, and strumming the guitar." Each phrase uses an *-ing* form of a verb and a direct object, aka a gerund phrase. In contrast, this sentence does not use parallel phrases: "Ralph loves playing football, to sketch portraits, and the guitar." The three items in the list are a gerund phrase (see the *-ing*?), an infinitive phrase (see the *to* before the verb?), and a noun. Tell students that they don't have to worry about naming the type of phrase, but they do need to know how to recognize phrase structure so they can make the phrases parallel.

Just like words and phrases, clauses can be parallel in structure. Example: "If you love me, if you need me, if you trust me, then show it with your actions." All three clauses begin with the subordinate conjunction *if*. Other subordinate conjunctions are *when, who, whom, whenever, after, since,* and so on. Here's another example: "I think of you whenever I eat strawberries, whenever I dance to a slow song, and whenever I look at the stars." In contrast, this sentence does not use clauses with parallel structure: "I think of you whenever I eat strawberries, times when a slow song plays, and sitting outside under the stars." (Note: You may need to break the lesson here and continue the next day.)

4. **Small-Group Activity**: Organize students into groups of five, and pass out copies of the handout. Have students divide the responsibilities to complete the handout. For example, each student could complete one of the five items, and then the group as a whole can check each person's work and make corrections. As they do so, each person can complete the remaining four items on the handout.

5. **Wrap-Up**: As homework, have students take out a piece of writing that they are working on for a class or that they previously completed for a class (teacher's choice). They should go through the piece looking for errors in parallel structure or opportunities to use parallel structure. They should make revisions to their pieces and then submit a report to you in which they give examples of the parallel structures that they used.

Extend the Lesson

- Have students bring in an example of parallel structure that they find in a published work of literature or nonfiction. They can look in a novel or magazine that they're reading, for example, or search blogs and Op-Ed pieces on a reputable website such as the *Washington Post* (www.washingtonpost.com) or the *New York Times* (www.nytimes.com). Have students share their example with the full class or in small groups, identifying whether the parallel structure uses words, phrases, or clauses. As they search, students may come across examples of botched parallel structure— tell them that errors in parallelism are more common than they might expect! You might encourage them to bring those in and show the class how to revise the samples to use parallel structure.

Differentiation

For students who need extra support

- Before assigning the challenging handout included with this lesson plan, assign (or walk students through) a less-challenging work sheet such as the one from ASU listed in the additional resources section.

- During the following activity for advanced students, ask one or more struggling students to serve as scribes to write examples and make corrections on the board. This gives these students an active role in the class activity without putting them on the spot. In addition, by writing and correcting examples of parallel structure, they go through the physical process of manipulating words, phrases, and clauses.

For advanced students

During the mini-lesson, ask volunteers to create example sentences using parallel structure. Even if students make mistakes in structure, you can use it as a teaching opportunity. You might say, "This is a solid example of parallel structure except for this one item. How can we revise it to make it fit with the structure of the other items?" (Notice that the pronoun *we* shifts the focus off the student who made the mistake and back to the class, placing the responsibility with the group.) After verifying that the sentence is correct or corrected, thank the student who provided it. "Thank you, Tyrone, for that example. Who wants to create the next example?"

Assessment

You can assign a score to the handout by assigning one point to each correctly completed item, with item 5 (the revision) being worth two points, for a top score of 6.

Additional Resources

- The Purdue Online Writing Lab has a mini-lesson on parallel structure: http://owl.english.purdue.edu/owl/resource/623/1/.

- Students at Arizona State University created this one-page lesson and one-page practice work sheet on parallel structure: http://english.clas.asu.edu/files/shared/enged/ParallelStructure.pdf.

Notes

After implementing the lesson, reflect on what worked and what you would change the next time.

_____

_____

_____

_____

Identify Parallel Structure

1. Read this excerpt from an article about pets and heat safety by Laura Blue. Underline two lists that use parallel parts of speech. (Hint: They both use nouns.)

Watch for these signs: heavy panting, collapse or staggering, drooling, vomiting, lethargy, glassy eyes, rapid heartbeat and, naturally (since the condition is caused by overheating), unusually high body temperature. Very old pets, very young ones and the overweight are at the greatest risk, and certain breeds with short noses—think pugs, boxers and bulldogs among dogs, and Persians and exotics among cats—will have more trouble with the heat because they can't pant as well, according to Petfinder.com.

—from "6 Ways to Keep Your Pets Safe in the Heat"

2. Read this excerpt from an Op-Ed piece by Joel Achenbach. Underline the two sets of parallel phrases. (Hint: One set is prepositional phrases; the other set is noun phrases.)

Bad Information does not happen by accident. It is promulgated. The sources are increasingly sophisticated. Today, almost everyone has advanced technology for disseminating data, from Web sites to phone banks to cable TV infomercials; everyone has a private public relations staff and a private media relations staff and a private Scientific Advisory Panel to lend "expert" authority to implausible assertions.

—from "The Age of Bad Information"

3. Read this excerpt from a short story by Nicholasa Mohr. Underline the two sets of parallel phrases.

He was nine when he became head of the household. Sometimes he would get work in the fields or at the sugar refinery, working from sun-up to sundown, bringing home twenty-five, maybe thirty cents a day. . . . Other days he would work chopping wood, running errands, and cleaning the hog pens, to be paid in food; but enough so that they wouldn't starve at home.

—from "A Time with a Future (Carmela)"

4. Read this excerpt from a speech by President John F. Kennedy. Underline the three sets of parallel clauses.

The heart of the question is whether all Americans are to be afforded equal rights and equal opportunities, whether we are going to treat our fellow Americans as we want to be treated. If an American, because his skin is dark, cannot eat lunch in a restaurant open to the public, if he cannot send his children to the best public school available, if he cannot vote for the public officials who will represent him, if, in short, he cannot enjoy the full and free life which all of us want, then who among us would be content to have the color of his skin changed and stand in his place? Whom among us would then be content with the counsels of patience and delay?

—from "Report to the American People on Civil Rights, 11 June 1963"

5. Read this excerpt from an article on kids and sleep by Alexandra Sifferlin. Look at the underlined items in the list. How could you revise the items so that they all have parallel structure? On the lines that follow, rewrite the list to show parallel structure.

Researchers assessed children's sleep quality by using portions of a standard questionnaire measuring <u>how often kids have trouble falling asleep</u>, <u>their nightmare frequency</u>, <u>how many times they wake up during the night</u>, <u>their difficulty waking up in the morning</u> and <u>how tired they are during the day</u>. The questionnaires were administered at the start of the study and again at 6, 12 and 18 months. At the start of the study, there weren't any significant differences between the two groups in terms of sleep problems or TV habits. The most common problem kids had was trouble falling asleep, with 38% of kids taking more than 20 minutes to fall asleep at least a couple of nights a week.

—from "Stick to *Sesame Street*: Violent TV Disrupts Kids' Sleep"

Your revision of the list:

_____

_____

_____

_____

_____

Everything in Its Place

MLA Style

Grade Levels: 9–10

Time Frame: Approximately one or two class periods

Overview: This lesson involves students in an active discovery and practice of putting MLA style into practice in their own work. You can use this lesson in conjunction with any writing assignment that requires students to quote or paraphrase print or online sources.

Common Core State Standards

- 9–10: Language, Standard 3: Apply knowledge of language to understand how language functions in different contexts, to make effective choices for meaning and style, and to comprehend more fully when reading or listening. a. Write and edit work so that it conforms to the guidelines in a style manual (e.g., *MLA Handbook*, Turabian's *Manual for Writers*) appropriate for the discipline and writing type.

Objectives

- Students will review the *MLA Handbook*'s guidelines for including and formatting in-text citations of sources and works-cited pages.

- Students will edit one of their own works-in-progress to show correct MLA style.

Background Knowledge Required

- Students should be in the process of writing an informative or argumentative piece that uses direct quotations from source materials. Ideally, each student should have a couple of different quotations or paraphrases from different sources to work with.

- Students should know the meaning of the term *plagiarism*.

Materials Needed

- Copies of students' drafts of informative or argumentative pieces. Remind them the day before to bring them in.

- One or more copies of the *MLA Handbook for Writers of Research Papers*. See chapter 5, "Documenting and Preparing the List of Works Cited," and chapter 6, "Documentation: Citing Sources in the Text."

Agenda

1. **Introduction**: To focus students' attention on the "why" of documenting sources, open class with a short narrative about a famous plagiarism scandal. Here is an example:

   > Once upon a time, there was a famous author. He worked as a history professor for 35 years, and he decided to write historical biographies and novels. Some of his most well known novels are *Band of Brothers*, *D-Day*, *Citizen Soldiers*, and *The Wild Blue*. In 1998, he received the National Humanities Medal, and in 2001 *Band of Brothers* was made into a television miniseries. This author was famous and popular and admired. Then one day, he was accused of plagiarism. Critic after critic started pointing out examples of other authors' exact words he had copied into his novels without putting them in quotation marks or citing the source. In the end, critics identified plagiarism in seven of his books. This author is Stephen E. Ambrose. While his novels are still popular, his reputation is permanently tarnished. This author did not live happily ever after. He died in 2002 during the firestorm of his plagiarism scandal.

   Build on the topic of plagiarism by reminding students that, as they know, responsible writers cite the sources of information they use in their writing. Responsible writers cite direct quotations *and* paraphrased ideas. One way of citing sources is by following guidelines in the *MLA Handbook*.

2. **In-Text Citations**: Ask students to take out the drafts they are working on. Ask them to find places in their papers where they quote or paraphrase another author's words or ideas. How do they cite their sources? Ask a volunteer to write a short example on the board, demonstrating the use of quotation marks, the parenthetical citation of author's last name and page number, and the sentence's end punctuation. Help the student correct the example if necessary. Get a few more volunteers to demonstrate examples from their work, making sure to include at least one example of paraphrased source material. If no one volunteers a paraphrase, use an existing example to create a paraphrase, showing that, except for the quotation marks, there is no difference in the ways of citing the source. (You may want to break the lesson here and continue the next day.)

3. **Works-Cited Page**: Tell students that, as they know, the in-text citations refer to the master list of works cited at the end of the paper or book. The *MLA Handbook* asks writers to title this list Works Cited. The handbook provides guidelines for what information to include in each entry. Ask volunteers to work with you to write sample entries on the board to demonstrate the correct format of entries for books, websites, magazine articles, newspaper articles, and other types of sources that students have used. Here are some examples, taken from the *MLA Handbook*. The bracketed boldfaced explanations have been added to explain the type of entry, for teaching purposes.

   Works Cited
   Allende, Isabel. "Toad's Mouth." Trans. Margaret Sayers Peden. *A Hammock beneath the Mangoes: Stories from Latin America*. Ed. Thomas Colchie. New York: Plume, 1992. 83–88. Print. **[story in an anthology, including**

story translator's name, anthology editor's name, and inclusive page numbers of story]

Eaves, Morris, Robert Essick, and Joseph Viscomi, eds. *The William Blake Archive*. Lib. of Cong., 28 Sept. 2007. Web. 20 Nov. 2007. http://www .blakearchive.org/blake/. **[website; note that the URL is required only if others' would have a hard time finding the website using search terms alone]**

Gergen, David. "A Question of Values." Editorial. *U.S. News and World Report* 11 Feb. 2002: 72. Print. **[editorial; a letter to the editor is formatted the same way but with the word *Letter* in place of the word *Editorial*]**

Harbord, Janet. *The Evolution of Film: Rethinking Film Studies*. Cambridge, UK: Polity, 2007. Print. **[standard book citation]**

Hutcheon, Linda, and Michael Hutcheon. *Bodily Charm: Living Opera*. Lincoln: U of Nebraska P, 2000. Print. **[book with two authors]**

"It Barks! It Kicks! It Scores!" *Newsweek* 30 July 2001: 12. Print. **[article with no author given]**

Piper, Andrew. "Rethinking the Print Object: Goethe and the Book of Everything." *PMLA* 121.1 (2006): 124–38. Print. **[article in scholarly journal]**

Tyre, Peg. "Standardized Tests in College?" *Newsweek*. Newsweek, 16 Nov. 2007. Web. 15 May 2008. **[article on website, including date of publication on web and date of access; note that in this example, the URL is not included]**

Wood, Jason. "Spellbound." *Sight and Sound* Dec. 2005: 28–30. Print. **[magazine article]**

4. **Wrap-Up**: As homework, have students edit their drafts to show correct format of in-text citations and a works-cited page that uses correct format. (If there is time remaining in class, they can start this work independently or with partners.)

Differentiation

For students who need extra support

- Plan class time to help students workshop their in-text citations or works-cited pages, either one-on-one or in small groups with similar needs.

For advanced students

- Consider appointing advanced students as workshop leaders for the activity listed above for students who need extra support.

Assessment

- Review students' drafts for accuracy of in-text citations and works-cited pages. Mark mistakes, and ask students to revise before turning in the final draft.

Additional Resources

- The Purdue Online Writing Lab has an excellent and student-friendly set of pages titled "MLA Formatting and Style Guide": owl.english.purdue.edu/owl/resource/ 747/01. Students can click on items in the menu at the left to get information about how to cite specific kinds of sources.

Notes

After implementing the lesson, reflect on what worked and what you would change the next time.

_____

_____

_____

_____

If You Don't Get This Lesson, Explain It to Me

Understanding Paradox

Grade Levels: 11–12

Time Frame: Approximately one or two class periods

Overview: This lesson teaches students to understand how paradox is used in informational and literary texts. The texts used are *The Paradox of Choice*, by Barry Schwartz, and *Hamlet*, by William Shakespeare; however, you can implement this lesson with texts of your own choosing.

Common Core State Standards

- 11–12: Language, Standard 5: Demonstrate understanding of figurative language, word relationships, and nuances in word meanings. a. Interpret figures of speech (e.g., hyperbole, paradox) in context and analyze their roles in text.

- 11–12: Writing, Standard 10: Write routinely over extended time frames . . . and shorter time frames . . . for a range of tasks, purposes, and audiences.

Objectives

- Students will understand why authors might use a paradox.

- Students will find examples of paradoxes in a text.

- Students will analyze how a paradox is different from an oxymoron.

Background Knowledge Required

Students should be familiar with the definition of *oxymoron*. The language standards for grades 9 and 10 have students interpret oxymorons as well as euphemisms. Students should have read up to act 3 of *Hamlet*.

Materials Needed

- Copies of the prologue from *The Paradox of Choice*

- Copies of *Hamlet*

Agenda

1. **Introduction and Independent Reading**: Pass out copies of the prologue from *The Paradox of Choice*. Tell students that their goal is to read it and try to understand

what a paradox might be. In the prologue, Schwartz reveals the paradox that his book will discuss but never explicitly uses the term *paradox* or defines it, so students will have to infer what the term might mean.

2. **Full-Class Discussion**: When students are done reading, have them share what they think the paradox is and what a paradox might mean. Write some of their comments on the board and agree on a definition of a paradox as a class (formal definition of a paradox: a figure of speech in which a statement or phrase appears to contradict itself). Ask students to come up with other examples of paradoxes in their lives or in the world around them. (Note: You may need to break the lesson here and continue the next day.)

3. **Independent Work**: Have students open their copies of *Hamlet*. Tell students that a famous example of a paradox is Hamlet's line, "I must be cruel only to be kind." What might that mean, and what does it reveal about Hamlet's character? Have students write paragraphs reflecting on that line.

4. **Wrap-Up**: Tell students that as they continue reading *Hamlet*, they should continue to look for examples of paradoxes and jot them in a notebook. You will discuss them in class.

Extend the Lesson

- Briefly review irony and oxymorons. Have students distinguish among those devices and paradoxes. Students can create a guide of literary devices that reviews all of the terms they have learned so far and explains how each one is different. The guide should include examples for each device and can be done as a collaborative class wiki.

Differentiation

For students who need extra support
- Give students literary examples of paradoxes before having them find their own examples in *Hamlet*.

For advanced students
- Have students help their peers identify paradoxes as they read.

Assessment

- Check students' paragraphs to make sure they understand what a paradox is and what that paradox reveals about Hamlet.

- If you extend the lesson, assess students' literary guides to make sure they are able to distinguish among the different literary devices.

Additional Resources

- This lesson teaches paradox using *Macbeth* instead of *Hamlet*: www.folger.edu/eduLesPlanDtl.cfm?lpid=801.http://teachers.net/lessons/posts/3509.html.

Notes

After implementing the lesson, reflect on what worked and what you would change the next time.

_____

_____

_____

_____

Are Those Words Working Together?

Using Hyphens Correctly

Lesson Plan 33

Grade Levels: 11–12

Time Frame: Approximately one class period

Overview: This lesson teaches students about a more sophisticated punctuation mark—the hyphen. Students will learn when and why to use it. They will then apply this lesson to text-based or research-based essays they are working on in class.

Common Core State Standards

- 11–12: Language, Standard 2: Demonstrate command of the conventions of standard English capitalization, punctuation, and spelling when writing. a. Observe hyphenation conventions.

- 11–12: Writing, Standard 5: Develop and strengthen writing as needed by planning, revising, editing, rewriting, or trying a new approach, focusing on addressing what is most significant for a specific purpose and audience. (Editing for conventions should demonstrate command of Language standards 1–3 up to and including grades 11–12 on page 54.)

Objectives

- Students will learn the general guidelines for proper hyphen use.

- Students will use hyphens correctly in their own writing.

Background Knowledge Required

Students should be familiar with the parts of speech.

Materials Needed

- Copies of essays that students are working on for your class or for another class. Remind them the day before to bring them in.

Agenda

1. **Introduction**. Put these two sentences on the board, and ask students if there's a difference in meaning.

   The chocolate covered almonds are on the table.
   The chocolate-covered almonds are on the table.

In the first example, you could mean chocolate almonds that are covered by plastic wrap or some such. In the second example, it's clear that you mean the almonds are covered in chocolate. Explain to students that writers use hyphens to join two adjectives that modify the same noun. They are called compound adjectives.

2. **Mini-Lesson**: Have students come up with other examples of compound adjectives. Point out that the rule is sometimes subjective and that the English language constantly evolves. Sometimes people do not use hyphens for very commonly used terms. For example, the *thank-you* in *thank-you note* should be hyphenated, but many people no longer do so. "High school students" is usually not hyphenated, but yet "college-ready students" would be hyphenated. As with other grammar rules, people have to know the rules but also use their own judgment.

   Go over other common hyphen uses, such as with ages and numbers. Also point out that there is sometimes hyphenation within a word, such as mini-lesson. When students are not sure about in-word hyphenation, they can consult a dictionary or style guide.

3. **Independent Work**: Have students go back to their essays and check for proper use of hyphens. If they did not include any compound adjectives in their writing, have them go back and incorporate at least three examples for practice.

4. **Wrap-Up**: Have students swap their essays with partners for feedback on their hyphenation use.

Extend the Lesson
- Explain how a hyphen is different from an en dash.

Differentiation
For students who need extra support
- Have students focus on only one hyphenation rule at a time. Provide them with more examples of the rule.

For advanced students
- Require more sophisticated use of hyphens in their writing.

Assessment
- Include correct use of hyphens on the rubric you use to assess students' essays.

Additional Resources
- The Grammar Girl site has these great pages about the rules for using hyphens:

  http://grammar.quickanddirtytips.com/grammar-hyphens.aspx
  http://grammar.quickanddirtytips.com/are-you-using-hyphens-correctly.aspx

Notes

After implementing the lesson, reflect on what worked and what you would change the next time.

_____

_____

_____

_____

Know When to Break the Rules

Issues of Complex or Contested Usage

Lesson Plan 34

Grade Levels: 11–12

Time Frame: Approximately one or two class periods

Overview: As students near the end of high school, many of them have begun to notice that published writers don't always follow the rules of grammar that students learn in school. Other rules of usage, (such as avoiding sexist language, are notoriously difficult to adhere to. Relying heavily on usage handbooks, this lesson helps students explore why writers might break grammar rules and which rules are more flexible than others.

Common Core State Standards

- 11–12: Language, Standard 1: Demonstrate command of the conventions of standard English grammar and usage when writing or speaking. a. Apply the understanding that usage is a matter of convention, can change over time, and is sometimes contested. b. Resolve issues of complex or contested usage, consulting references (e.g., *Merriam-Webster's Dictionary of English Usage, Garner's Modern American Usage*) as needed.

- 11–12: Writing, Standard 5: Develop and strengthen writing as needed by planning, revising, editing, rewriting, or trying a new approach, focusing on addressing what is most significant for a specific purpose and audience.

- 11–12: Speaking and Listening, Standard 1: Initiate and participate effectively in a range of collaborative discussions . . . with diverse partners on *grades 11–12 topics, texts, and issues,* building on others' ideas and expressing their own clearly and persuasively.

Objectives

- Students will examine examples of complex and contested conventions of grammar.

- Students will make informed decisions to resolve issues of complex or contested usage.

- Students will use a variety of reference sources to make informed decisions about usage.

Background Knowledge Required

Students should have a basic understanding of the rules of grammar usage to use as a point of reference in the discussion of complex or contested usage.

Materials Needed

- Six copies of usage handbooks. See suggested titles in agenda item 3. They do not all have to be the same title—in fact, a mix of titles would be great.

- Copies of the handout: Decipher Complex Conventions of Grammar Usage, p. 160

Agenda

1. **Introduction**: To generate student interest, write the following phrase on the board: "Knowing the rules–and when to break them." Introduce the topic of grammar by acknowledging the fact that, by grade 11 or 12, students have spent at least a decade learning the rules of grammar and how to use them to write, revise, and edit. They've spent a decade learning the rules. Now they are going to learn about some rules of grammar that can be broken for the right reasons. Making informed decisions to break rules of grammar is the privilege of well-trained, advanced writers. Tell students that if they do it awkwardly, their writing will look messy and unrevised. If they do it well, they will add a pleasing note to their personal writing style.

2. **Representative Example**: Write the phrase "sentence fragment" on the board, and then ask a volunteer to explain what that is. (Answer: a group of words punctuated as a sentence yet lacking a subject, a verb, or both.) Ask students to think about what they have learned about using sentence fragments in their writing. Have they been taught to leave them there or to revise them to create complete sentences?

   Explain that the standard rule of grammar is that a sentence fragment is a grammatical error—and this *is* true. However, once students know how to recognize sentence fragments, they can move on to learning when it's OK to use one. Yes! Use a sentence fragment! Ask for ideas about when it is and is not acceptable to use sentence fragments in writing. Examples might be that formal writing (such as book reports, essays, test answers, and other academic pieces) should not have sentence fragments. Informal writing and fiction may sometimes use fragments for effect— to make a character's dialogue sound real, for example, or to establish an informal or friendly tone.

3. **Authoritative Resources**: Remind students that when they have questions about the rules of grammar, they can consult a grammar handbook. Likewise, when they have questions about when breaking a rule of grammar is OK, they can consult a usage handbook. *Usage* is simply a reference to the usage of grammar. Have students write down the following bibliographic information for these authoritative usage handbooks. As a side note, you might point out that the format of these entries conforms to MLA style for a works-cited page. (These are just suggestions; feel free to use other handbooks or additional ones.)

   > Garner, Bryan A. *Garner's Modern American Usage*. 3rd edition. New York: Oxford University Press, 2009. Print.
   > ———. *Oxford Dictionary of American Usage and Style*. New York: Oxford University Press, 2000. Print.
   > Merriam-Webster. *Merriam-Webster's Dictionary of English Usage*. Springfield, MA: Merriam-Webster, 1994. Print.

4. **Small-Group Activity**: (This may take more than one class period.) Write the following topics on the board:

   - beginning a sentence with a coordinating conjunction such as *and* or *but*
   - incomplete sentences
   - sexist language
   - split infinitive
   - dangling participle
   - passive voice

   Organize students into six groups, and assign one topic per group. The topics are listed in the order of least to most complex; this may help you make decisions about forming groups and assigning topics. Have each group look up its assigned topic in a usage handbook. Students should quickly figure out that the handbooks are organized alphabetically by key term, as in a dictionary. Distribute the handout. Each group should prepare a summary of its findings to present to the class, using the handout to organize the information.

5. **Wrap-Up**: Have each group share its findings with the class. Students should take notes on the findings of the other five groups.

Extend the Lesson

- Include the complex-usage issue of words often confused. Here is a partial list of words:

affect, effect	infer, imply	verbal, oral
aggravate, irritate	it, it's	who, whom
alot, a lot	less, fewer	which, that
assure, ensure, insure	like, as or as if	prophecy, prophesy
disinterested, uninterested	their, there, they're	principal, principle

- Have students create podcasts that teach a rule of grammar and when, or if, it's OK to break it. For examples of podcasts on grammar rules, see the additional resources section.

Differentiation

For students who need extra support

- If students are fuzzy on the basic rule of their assigned usage issue, provide additional reference sources such as grammar handbooks, grammar glossaries, or access to an online handbook or glossary.

- Break the small-group activity into two days, with multiple groups on each day working on the same topic. Spend more time with groups, helping them figure out how to find the information they need in the dictionary entries. Groups working on the same topic can co-present their findings by taking turns, item by item on the handout, and by adding to and commenting on the other groups' information.

For advanced students

- Allow students to work in smaller groups, a technique that places a greater burden of responsibility for completing the handout on each group member.

- Encourage these students to provide their own examples, in addition to the handbook's, in items 4 and 6 on the handout.

- If you have extra usage handbooks, allow advanced students to consult more than one handbook to gather information for their handouts.

Assessment

Have students write blog entries directed at high-school students. They should explain which rule of grammar they plan to break, when it is appropriate, and why. Encourage students to actually break that rule of grammar in their blog entries. You can use the following rubric to assess the blog entries, performance in the lesson, or both.

Student's grasp of a handful of complex or contested issues of usage is

score 4	advanced
score 3	proficient
score 2	rudimentary
score 1	flawed
score 0	absent

Additional Resources

- The Texas A&M University Writing Center has posted online podcasts that teach grammar basics related to some of the topics in this lesson, including modifiers, passive and active voice, and biased (sexist) language: writingcenter.tamu.edu/c/podcasts.

Notes

After implementing the lesson, reflect on what worked and what you would change the next time.

_____

_____

_____

_____

Name: _____ Date: _____

Decipher Complex Conventions of Grammar Usage

Refer to a usage handbook to find out information on a topic of complex or contested grammar usage. Record your findings in the categories below.

1. Complex or contested topic of grammar usage:	

2. Definition of key terms (for example, what is an infinitive?):	

3. Standard rule of grammar for this topic:	**4.** Example(s) from the handbook or from your own knowledge:
5. What is complex or contested about this rule of grammar? Is it OK to break this rule of grammar for a specific purpose? If so, when or why?	**6.** Example(s) of acceptable breaking of the rule:

7. In your own writing, how will you make use of this rule of grammar and the possibility of breaking the rule?	

Notice Me! Notice Me!

Vary Syntax for Effect

Grade Levels: 11–12

Time Frame: Approximately one or two class periods

Overview: This lesson reviews techniques for varying the syntax in sentences, asking students to analyze the syntax of other writers as well as the syntax in their own writing. You can use the information in this lesson to create several mini-lessons simply by selecting a few techniques to cover at a time. Students can apply what they learn to any piece of writing they are working on for this or other classes.

Common Core State Standards

- 11–12: Language, Standard 3: Apply knowledge of language to understand how language functions in different contexts, to make effective choices for meaning or style, and to comprehend more fully when reading or listening. a. Vary syntax for effect, consulting references (e.g., Tufte's *Artful Sentences*) for guidance as needed; apply an understanding of syntax to the study of complex texts when reading.

- 11–12: Writing, Standard 5: Develop and strengthen writing as needed by planning, revising, editing, rewriting, or trying a new approach, focusing on addressing what is most significant for a specific purpose and audience.

- 11–12: Writing, Standard 10: Write routinely over extended time frames . . . and shorter time frames . . . for a range of tasks, purpose, and audiences.

- 11–12: Speaking and Listening, Standard 1: Initiate and participate effectively in a range of collaborative discussions . . . with diverse partners on *grades 11–12 topics, texts, and issues*, building on others' ideas and expressing their own clearly and persuasively.

Objectives

- Students will learn techniques for varying the syntax in sentences.

- Students will analyze the syntax of complex fictional and informational texts.

- Students will revise pieces of their own writing to demonstrate varied syntax.

Background Knowledge Required

Students should have a basic understanding of what phrases and clauses are.

Materials Needed

- Copies of the handout: Analyze Syntax in Complex Texts, p. 165

- Copies of basic and varied syntax, which follow (optional)

Agenda

1. **Introduction**: On the board, write the following:

   Notice me! Notice me!
   The Girl (or Boy) Who Stood Out in a Crowd

   Then, ask students to take five minutes to write a description, a narrative, or an opinion piece inspired by the words on the board.

2. **Full-Class Discussion**: Ask a few volunteers to read their pieces aloud. Direct students' attention to the theme of standing out in a crowd. Why would someone want to do this? How might a person do this? Students may suggest, for example, that a person might want to stand out from the crowd in order to be noticed, to feel set apart as special, to express individual style, or just to be different. Students' ideas for how a person might do this may range from using clothes, hairstyle, jewelry, and other personal touches to using surprising or outrageous behavior to be noticed.

3. **Mini-Lesson**: Link the theme of standing out from the crowd to personal writing style. You might say, "What does standing out from the crowd have to do with writing? Everything! Just as a person can stand out in a sea of people, you can make your writing stand out in a sea of other writing. How? By using the syntax of your sentences to say, 'Notice me! Notice me!' Syntax is simply the arrangement of words, phrases, and clauses to form sentences. One writer may use short, simple syntax; another writer may use long, convoluted syntax. Can you imagine how these two writers' styles would be different? You wouldn't mistake one for the other."

   On the board, write *subject-verb-object* and explain that this is the basic pattern of English sentences. Examples: "Spiderman climbed a tall building." "The cow jumped over the moon." This is basic, or usual, syntax. Explain that as writers become more sophisticated—and as they write for more sophisticated readers—they vary their syntax to create interesting sentences that don't all sound the same. Demonstrate by displaying (or passing out copies) of the following example. Ask students to point out how the second version uses varied syntax.

   Basic Syntax:
   Paulo went to the pet supplies store. He bought dog food, a metal dish, and a squeaky toy. He walked quickly down the sidewalk. He stopped at the bus stop on the corner. The bus rolled down the street in a huff of dank air. Paulo stepped onto the bus and sat down. He could not wait to pick up his new dog at the animal shelter.

   Varied Syntax:
   When Paulo went to the pet supplies store, he bought essentials: dog food, a metal dish, a squeaky toy. Then, moving quickly, he walked to the corner bus

stop where his ride was just rolling in on a huff of dank air. Stepping onto the bus, he sat down. "One hour!" he told himself. "One hour, and the shelter will have one less dog."

Move on to explain that there are reliable techniques for creating varied syntax in writing. Here are some tried and true methods:

- Begin the sentence with an introductory word, phrase, or clause.
- Use interrupting phrases set off by commas.
- Use appositives and nonrestrictive clauses, which are set off by commas.
- Use a question, an exclamation, or a command to vary a string of declarative sentences.
- Place a short sentence among longer ones and vice versa.
- Use varied punctuation to put words, phrases, and clauses together in the sentence. For example, use colons before lists. Use dashes to set off abrupt breaks in thought. Use parenthesis to add brief explanations or qualifiers.
- *Occasionally* break traditional rules of grammar, and begin a sentence with a coordinating conjunction (*and, but, yet*).

4. **Shared-Revision Activity**: Ask students to pair up. Their job is to work together to revise their written pieces about the girl (or boy) who stood out from the crowd. They should use at least two techniques from the list above. (Note: You may want to end the lesson here and continue the next day.)

5. **Wrap-Up**: Have students complete the handout. Follow up by reviewing and discussing students' responses on the handout.

Extend the Lesson

- Have students bring in the drafts of a piece of writing that they are working on for this or another class. Have them work independently or with partners to revise the pieces for varied syntax.

Differentiation

For students who need extra support

- Ask students to bring in samples of texts that they choose to read outside of school. They could print a web page, for example, or bring in a magazine. If they say that they don't read outside of class, ask them to go to the school or local library and check out books or magazines that interest them and bring them in. Have students analyze the syntax in one or more paragraphs of their chosen texts. Repeat this exercise at points throughout the year, helping students build to reading more sophisticated texts.

For advanced students

- Use the activity for students who need extra support, but encourage advanced students to have fun finding two or three different texts that use different kinds of syntax. For instance, Edgar Allan Poe's writing style is vastly different from Ernest Hemingway's. Ask students to consider how the authors' use of syntax helps create such contrasts.

Assessment

- Evaluate the results of the shared-revision activity. On a 4-point scale, award one point for each example of syntax that varies from the subject-verb-object structure.

Additional Resources

- As a reference source on varied syntax, the Common Core State Standards recommend Virginia Tufte's *Artful Sentences: Syntax as Style*. However, you can also find information, models, and practice exercises in many grammar handbooks by looking up the topic "sentence variety." *The Hodges Harbrace Handbook*, 18th edition, is one example, but older editions of this and other handbooks are equally useful.

Notes

After implementing the lesson, reflect on what worked and what you would change the next time.

_____

_____

_____

_____

Name: _____   Date: _____

Analyze Syntax in Complex Texts

Read each excerpt. After each one, list three techniques the writer used to create varied syntax, and tell which sentence uses the technique. The sentences have been numbered for easy reference.

Excerpt 1

¹*What* was going on? ²A roar of laughter from the aphasia ward, just as the President's speech was coming on, and they had all been so eager to hear the President speaking. . . .

³There he was, the old Charmer, the Actor, with his practiced rhetoric, his histrionisms, his emotional appeal—and all the patients were convulsed with laughter. ⁴Well, not all: some looked bewildered, some looked outraged, one or two looked apprehensive, but most looked amused. ⁵The President was, as always, moving—but he was moving them, apparently, mainly to laughter. ⁶What could they be thinking? ⁷Were they failing to understand him? ⁸Or did they, perhaps, understand him all too well?

—from *The Man Who Mistook His Wife for a Hat and Other Clinical Tales*, by Oliver Sacks

1. Varied syntax technique: _____

_____

_____

_____

2. Varied syntax technique: _____

_____

_____

_____

3. Varied syntax technique: _____

_____

_____

_____

Excerpt 2

¹It was raining that morning, and still very dark. ²When the boy reached the streetcar café he had almost finished his route and he went in for a cup of coffee. ³The place was an all-night café owned by a bitter and stingy man called Leo. ⁴After the raw, empty street, the café seemed friendly and bright; along the counter there were a couple of soldiers, three spinners from the cotton mill, and in a corner a man who sat hunched over with his nose and half his face down in a beer mug. ⁵The boy wore a helmet such as aviators wear. ⁶When he went into the café he unbuckled the chin strap and raised the right flap up over his pink little ear; often as he drank his coffee someone would speak to him in a friendly way. ⁷But this morning Leo did not look into his face and none of the men were talking. ⁸He paid and was leaving the café when a voice called out to him:

—from "A Tree, A Rock, A Cloud," by Carson McCullers

4. Varied syntax technique: _____

_____

_____

_____

5. Varied syntax technique: _____

_____

_____

_____

6. Varied syntax technique: _____

_____

_____

_____

Selecting Rich, Complex Texts for Student Reading

Grades 9–12

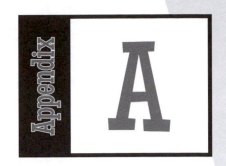

A variety of resources are available in your search for rich, complex texts for student reading. A few top-notch resources are the following:

- **American Library Association.** The ALA website has lists of book and media award winners that are on level for high-school readers. Go to the Book, Print, and Media Awards page, and in the menu at the left, select the subcategory Children & Young Adults. Examples are the Michael L. Printz Award, Outstanding Books for the College Bound and Lifelong Learners, Great Graphic Novels for Teens, Best Fiction for Young Adults, Alex Awards, Booklist Editor's Choice: Adult Books for Young Adults, Booklist Editor's Choice: Media, and Coretta Scott King Book Award. Go to www.ala.org/awardsgrants/awards/browse/bpma?showfilter=no.

- **Appendix B of the Common Core Standards for English Language Arts & Literacy in History/Social Studies, Science, and Technical Subjects.** The appendix lists nearly 140 exemplar texts grouped by genre for grades 9–10 and 11–12. It includes excerpts of each text. Literary authors range from Homer and Ovid to Shakespeare, Steinbeck, and U.S. presidents. Informational texts include topics in social studies, science, math, and technology. Go to www.corestandards.org/assets/Appendix_B.pdf. **Note:** These lists are merely suggestions and are in no way a mandatory or exclusive list of texts. Teachers should feel confident in choosing sources other than these exemplar texts.

- **EBSCO***host***.** Check to see if your school or public library subscribes to this searchable database. It includes full-text articles from magazines and newspapers as well as e-books and audio books. To see resources for high-school readers, go to http://ebscohost.com/us-high-schools.

- **The Horn Book.** *Horn Book Magazine* has short reviews (some starred) of current fiction, poetry and song, nonfiction, and audio books, with each review noting one or two reading levels: primary, intermediate, middle school, or high school. *Horn Book Guide* is a semiannual publication (print and online) that rates and reviews titles published in the previous six months, indexed for ease of use. Go to www.hbook.com.

- **The Junior Library Guild** creates lists of outstanding books, national and state award winners, and themes (e.g., black history, elections in the United States). Browsing the Guild's backlist of titles is also useful. You can sort the list by reading level and genre by using the advanced search feature. Go to www.juniorlibraryguild.com, click on Books & Levels, and then click on Backlist Catalog. Although the lists are aimed at librarians who want to expand their collections, they are equally useful to teachers.

- **Lexile Framework for Reading.** For lists of books that are leveled at grade level (or just below or just above), go to www.lexile.com, type in the grade you teach, choose book topics, and click Submit. You can sort for a wide range of topics, including biography, social issues, science and technology, graphic novels, and more. You can also type a book's title in the Quick Book Search box to find out its Lexile measure. For example, the measure for Henry David Thoreau's *Walden* is 1340L, which corresponds to a reading level beyond grade 12. Because the Common Core names *Walden* as a text exemplar for grades 11–12, you might choose to use a short excerpt of this text in a lesson built around reading and rereading for understanding. In contrast, texts with lower Lexile measures would be more suitable for independent and longer reading assignments.

- **Librarians.** Youth, aka teen or young-adult, librarians are usually enthusiastic about compiling lists of quality texts for teachers, given sufficient lead time. You might request nonfiction texts at a specific reading level, for example, or an assortment of fiction and nonfiction on a topic such as women's suffrage or natural disasters. You might need books or articles with maps, charts, diagrams, and timelines. Even if you don't need an entire reading list, librarians (who spend hours reading reviews of books in catalogs and journals) are happy to help you identify reputable texts that will serve a specific teaching purpose.

- **Library of Congress.** The LOC has online collections of historical newspapers, prints and photographs, sound recordings, maps, manuscripts, and primary source documents, all of which can help you meet requirements of the Common Core State Standards. Go to www.loc.gov/index.html to browse collections. Also, on that page, look for the "Especially for" menu, and click on Teachers. There you'll find primary source sets for classroom use and a link to the *Teaching with Primary Sources Journal*, available online.

- **Scholastic News Magazines.** Scholastic publishes classroom magazines leveled to student readers and correlated to Common Core standards. The texts increase in difficulty as the year progresses. *Scholastic Action, Choices, Scholastic Art,* and the *New York Times Upfront* are a few examples. Depending on the magazine, the texts are informational or incorporate a variety of text types and may include charts, graphs, maps, and links to online videos. Go to classroommagazines.scholastic.com to see all the magazines; look for the link to Common Core information.

- *School Library Journal.* Ask a school librarian if you can peruse a few copies of this monthly journal. The year-end Best Books issue is helpful. In any issue, flip to "The Book Review." Look for starred reviews in the subsections for Grades 5 & Up and Adult Books for High School Students. For example, in the December 2008 issue, a starred review recommends Michael T. Kaufman's *1968* for grades 9 and up. This nonfiction book has sections on the Tet Offensive, the Vietnam War, the assassinations of Martin Luther King Jr., and Robert Kennedy, and other worldwide topics. Each section includes photographs and a reproduced image of a front page from the *New York Times* (the full text of each article is appended). Elsewhere in each journal issue, a review article focuses on a single topic, such as the Arctic, and reviews numerous relevant websites, DVDs, fiction, and nonfiction.

- *Senior High Core Collection.* Ask a local librarian if you can peruse the library's copy of H. W. Wilson Publishing Company's *Senior High Core Collection.* This resource annotates and evaluates fiction, nonfiction, story collections, and magazines for high school readers. According to the company's website, "the books listed encompass a wide variety of topics for youth, ranging from material on Native Americans and rainforest ecology to health issues. Additional subject coverage includes biographies, art, sports, Islam, the Middle East, cultural diversity and other contemporary topics." **Note**: The word *core* in the title does not refer to the Common Core.

- **Smithsonian Institution.** The Smithsonian has online resources for educators, including curricula, print materials, multimedia, and videos for loan. Topics include American history, inventions and innovation, American art, African art, air and space, and more. Find the home page for educators at www.si.edu/Educators. In addition, the page for researchers has links to resources such as the *Encyclopedia Smithsonian*, an online encyclopedia suitable for student use. The Online Collections and Databases may also be of use. The research home page is at www.si.edu/Researchers.

- **State and regional library associations** sponsor book awards. For example, the Iowa Association of School Librarians sponsors the Iowa High School Book Award. Recent winners include books with a definite edge and complex themes, such as Suzanne Collins's *The Hunger Games* and Jay Asher's *Th1rteen R3asons Why*. Another example is the Young Readers Choice Awards, administered by the Pacific Northwest Library Association. See details at www.pnla.org/yrca/. A librarian at your school or local library can give you information on your state's or region's award program and help you find the book lists from other programs.

- **Young Adult Library Services Association** (YALSA) maintains lists of award-winning and notable books and media for readers ages 12 to 18. For example, the 2010 Fabulous Films for Young Adults list is themed "Outside In: Rebellion vs. Conformity" and includes *Freedom Writers* (2007), a film about a teacher in a racially divided school who teaches students to use writing as their voice. The Great Graphic Novels 2012 list includes the nonfiction title *The Influencing Machine: Brooke Gladstone on the Media* (2011), by Brooke Gladstone, Josh Neufeld, and others. The tagline is "How is the media telling you what to think?" YALSA's home page is www.ala.org/yalsa.

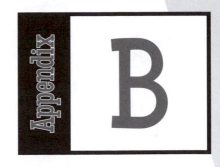
Sample Argument Writing Prompts

Grades 9–12

Although acknowledging the importance of informative and narrative writing, the Common Core introduces a new emphasis on argument writing in grades 9–12. The following writing prompts, organized by grade level, are intended to provide ideas and inspiration as you incorporate argument writing into your curriculum. For each grade band (9–10 and 11–12), a Checklist for Argument Writing is included following the writing prompts; the checklist is intended as a student handout to accompany each argument assignment.

Feel free to modify these samples to fit your teaching purposes. For instance, you may want to tailor a writing task to focus on one or two key skills of argument writing instead of focusing on every detail of the writing standard at once. Each grade band's argument-writing standard is included in full for easy reference.

To create your own prompts, keep this tip in mind: build the writing task around an arguable claim. Some claims are controversial; others are simply open to multiple interpretations or points of view. Either is fine. The essential quality is that a prompt be a statement or an idea that people can disagree about. Students should support the claim with evidence rather than appeals to the emotions of the reader (i.e., being persuasive), and they should address counterclaims.

You can create short writing tasks by having students write for five minutes in response to a pro-or-con, either-or, or yes-or-no prompt. An example is "Does the effort involved in cheating actually teach students the material?" Responses could be T-charts or freewriting. These quick tasks let students focus on articulating an arguable claim and identifying a supporting reason or two. In contrast, the longer writing tasks that follow require students to produce more sophisticated written responses.

Grades 9–10

Writing Standard 1: Write arguments to support claims in an analysis of substantive topics or texts, using valid reasoning and relevant and sufficient evidence.

a. Introduce precise claim(s), distinguish the claim(s) from alternate or opposing claims, and create an organization that establishes clear relationships among claim(s), counterclaims, reasons, and evidence.

b. Develop claim(s) and counterclaims fairly, supplying evidence for each while pointing out the strengths and limitations of both in a manner that anticipates the audience's knowledge level and concerns.

c. Use words, phrases, and clauses to link the major sections of the text, create cohesion, and clarify the relationships between claim(s) and reasons, between reasons and evidence, and between claim(s) and counterclaims.

d. Establish and maintain a formal style and objective tone while attending to the norms and conventions of the discipline in which they are writing.

e. Provide a concluding statement or section that follows from and supports the argument presented.

Grade 9

Writing Prompt 1

Context for Writing: This prompt works well in conjunction with reading a poem or narrative that demonstrates a rich use of figurative and connotative language.

Writing Task: Think about the narrative (poem) that you read. From your point of view, does the author's use of figurative and connotative language enhance or hinder the reader's understanding of the text? Write an argument to prove your claim about the language of the narrative (poem).

Writing Prompt 2

Context for Writing: Use this prompt following a discussion of a moral lesson or statement about society in a work of fiction or a biography. Make sure that students identify a lesson or statement as opposed to just a topic. For instance, a moral lesson is "A tragedy can destroy you, or it can make you leave your cocoon to become to butterfly"; a topic is "facing tragedy."

Writing Task: Think about the moral lesson or statement about society in the work you read. Does it accurately reflect the real world, or does it idealize or romanticize the real world? Write an argument to prove your claim about the text's theme.

Writing Prompt 3

Context for Writing: Have students read a book such as *To Kill a Mockingbird* and watch a film version of the book. Have students pre-write or have discussions in which they compare the effects of the elements used in each medium. Techniques might include characterization, dialogue, narrative voice, description, sound, camera angle, and others.

Writing Task: Write an argument in which you prove which version of the narrative is better, the book or the film.

Writing Prompt 4

Context for Writing: Have students research the topic of teens and jobs. What is the minimum age for employment? What are the pros and cons of holding a job while going to high school? Why might teens lie about their age to get a job before they're legally old enough?

Writing Task: Is it ever acceptable for a teenager to lie about his or her age to get a job before being legally old enough to work? Why or why not? Write an argument to prove your point of view on this topic.

Writing Prompt 5

Context for Writing: Use this prompt with a full-class discussion on the theme "room for improvement in our school." You might suggest topics such as nutrition, respect, fun, safety, cleanliness, or school spirit.

Writing Task: Think about what needs to improve at your school. Also consider ideas your classmates have expressed. Choose one thing you think most needs improvement. Who is responsible for implementing this improvement? Students? Teachers? The school administration? Everyone? Why? Write a letter to the student body, the teachers, and/or the principal to convince them to implement this change.

Grade 10

Writing Prompt 1

Context for Writing: Read and discuss a historical speech, such as Judge Learned Hand's speech for I Am an American Day, sometimes called the "Spirit of Liberty" speech. Choose a speech with a key idea that is debatable. Consider this example from Hand's speech:

> I often wonder whether we do not rest our hopes too much upon constitutions, upon laws, and upon courts. These are false hopes; believe me, these are false hopes. Liberty lies in the hearts of men and women; when it dies there, no constitution, no law, no court can save it; no constitution, no law, no court can even do much to help it. While it lies there, it needs no constitution, no law, no court to save it.
>
> —from the "Spirit of Liberty" speech, by Judge Learned Hand, www.providenceforum.org/spiritoflibertyspeech. Accessed August 17, 2012.

As a class, analyze the speech to identify the speaker's claim or main idea, and identify the reasons the speaker uses to support his claim.

Writing Task: Think about the author's claim in the speech you read and discussed. Do you agree or disagree with this claim? Why? Write an argument to convince your classmates that your point of view is correct.

Writing Prompt 2

Context for Writing: Use this prompt in conjunction with a full-class discussion on the topic of technology in classrooms. What kinds of technology do classrooms in your school need? What are the top three priorities? Why are they higher priorities than others?

Writing Task: From your point of view, what one type of technology *most* needs to be added to classrooms in your school? Write a letter to your principal to convince him or her that it's necessary to make this improvement in your school.

Writing Prompt 3

Context for Writing: Have students compare and contrast two or more accounts of a subject told in different mediums (e.g., a print biography and a biographic film or a written account of a historical event and a documentary about the event).

Writing Task: Think about the two accounts of the subject that you examined. Which account does a better job of presenting the information? Write an argument to prove your point of view.

Writing Prompt 4

Context for Writing: Have students read an opinion text such as an Op-Ed piece, a letter to the editor, or a blog. In a class discussion, determine the author's point of view on the topic and analyze how the author explained or defended the point of view.

Writing Task: Think about the opinion text that you read. Do you agree or disagree with the author's point of view? Write an argument to prove your point of view.

Writing Prompt 5

Context for Writing: Provide articles, or have students find informative sources, about banned books in high schools.

Writing Task: Is it acceptable for a school district to ban certain books in its classrooms? Or should teachers have full freedom to choose the books they teach? Write an argument to prove your point of view on this topic.

Name: _____   Date: _____

Checklist for Writing an Argument
Grades 9–10

Use this checklist to make sure you include the essential elements in the title, introduction, body, and conclusion of your argument.

- **Title**. Give your paper a title that identifies the topic, hints at your claim (such as asking a question that your claim answers), or expresses your claim outright. You might think of other ways to make your title informative *and* interesting.

- **Introductory Section**. Introduce the debatable topic and state your claim (your judgment, point of view, or opinion). If your claim is about a work of literature or other text, give the title and author of the work. Introduce these key elements in the order that best highlights your claim. You might choose to introduce an opposing claim in this section or wait until the body of your paper.

- **Body Paragraphs**. Develop your claim by explaining reasons and evidence that show your claim to be logical, valid, and defensible. Likewise, develop the opposing viewpoint by explaining its limitations objectively (no insults, sarcasm, or jokes). Show your understanding of the topic by carefully choosing facts, details, examples, and quotations to support your claim.

- **Writer's Craft**. To link ideas, sentences, and paragraphs clearly, use words and phrases that signal comparisons, contrasts, a cause-and-effect relationship, sequence, or add ons. Some examples are *similarly*, *in contrast*, *consequently*, *after that*, and *additionally*. Also, use standard English, sophisticated word choices, and correct grammar to create a formal writing style.

- **Conclusion**. In the conclusion statement or section, reinforce your claim with a final thought, a restatement of your claim, a summary of your strongest reasons, or a similar technique.

Grades 11–12

Writing Standard 1: Write arguments to support claims in an analysis of substantive topics or texts, using valid reasoning and relevant and sufficient evidence.

a. Introduce precise, knowledgeable claim(s), establish the significance of the claim(s), distinguish the claim(s) from alternate or opposing claims, and create an organization that logically sequences claim(s), counterclaims, reasons, and evidence.

b. Develop claim(s) and counterclaims fairly and thoroughly, supplying the most relevant evidence for each while pointing out the strengths and limitations of both in a manner that anticipates the audience's knowledge level, concerns, values, and possible biases.

c. Use words, phrases, and clauses as well as varied syntax to link the major sections of the text, create cohesion, and clarify the relationships between claim(s) and reasons, between reasons and evidence, and between claim(s) and counterclaims.

d. Establish and maintain a formal style and objective tone while attending to the norms and conventions of the discipline in which they are writing.

e. Provide a concluding statement or section that follows from and supports the argument presented.

Grade 11

Writing Prompt 1

Context for Writing: Have students research societal values in a period in U.S. history, perhaps in conjunction with reading a literary or an informational text that demonstrates or discusses values. For example, students could research Puritan values and read Hawthorne's "Young Goodman Brown." They could research Prohibition and read an excerpt from Frederick Lewis Allen's *Only Yesterday: An Informal History of the 1920s.*

Writing Task: Think about the societal values you examined. Does the society you live in today have the same values? Write an argument to prove your point of view on the subject.

Writing Prompt 2

Context for Writing: Have a full-class discussion about how students spend their free time on a typical weekend. Should every minute be scheduled for maximum fun? Should the television set stay turned off? Should the time be devoted to family and friends? What is the best use of a Saturday afternoon? Then have students research to answer a question such as "How much time, on average, does a high-school student spend watching television?" or "What percentage of high-school students play sports (or practice a musical instrument) in their spare time?" or "What percentage of high-school students read in their spare time?" Students may want to team up with someone writing on the same topic and perform the research task together.

Writing Task: Write a letter to your class as a whole. Use the letter to prove your point of view on the best way to spend a Saturday afternoon.

Writing Prompt 3

Context for Writing: Have students examine two or more mediums that present the same drama. Examples are a print text, a live performance, and a film.

Writing Task: Consider the different mediums that you examined. Which one did the best job of presenting the drama? Write an argument to prove your point of view.

Writing Prompt 4

Context for Writing: Have students read two or three news or magazine articles about social media. Conduct a full-class discussion about whether social media help or hinder the development and maintenance of deep friendships.

Writing Task: Do social media help or hinder the development and maintenance of deep friendships? Write an argument to prove your point of view.

Writing Prompt 5

Context for Writing: Have students read a historical speech or letter that sought to effect a particular change in a community, a society, or the world. In a class discussion, analyze the author's purpose in writing the text.

Writing Task: Think about the author's purpose in writing the persuasive text that you read. Did this speech help bring about the change the author envisioned? Why or why not? Write an argument to prove your judgment on the matter.

Grade 12

Writing Prompt 1

Context for Writing: Read accounts of protests that sought to effect, or inadvertently effected, change in a society. Examples are the Boston Tea Party, the sit-in of the Greensboro Four, the Tiananmen Square protests of 1989, and the Los Angeles riots in response to the decision in the case of Rodney King.

Writing Task: In protests to change a society, what should the roles of peace and violence be? Write an argument to prove your point of view.

Writing Prompt 2

Context for Writing: Ask students to discuss whether they still read fairy tales or watch film or cartoon versions of fairy tales. Ask questions such as "Which fairy tale was your favorite when you were young? Why?" and "Which fairy tale is your favorite now? Why?" and "Why do you think kids or young people or adults read fairy tales?"

Writing Task: Are fairy tales just for kids, or are they for people of all ages? Why? Write an argument to prove your point of view.

Writing Prompt 3

Context for Writing: Use this writing prompt in conjunction with reading a narrative from the 20th century or earlier that features a young protagonist. Examples are *The Catcher in the Rye, The Chocolate War, Lord of the Flies, The Outsiders, A Separate Peace, The Yearling,* and *The Adventures of Huckleberry Finn,*

Writing Task: Think about the main character and the main problem that he or she faced. Think about the details of the conflict and its solution. From your point of view, is this novel outdated, or are the character and plot relevant to the 2010s? Write an argument to prove your point of view.

Writing Prompt 4

Context for Writing: Identify a current hot topic, and have each student bring in an opinion or informational piece on the topic. In a class discussion, debate the issue, drawing on ideas and evidence in the texts (e.g., opinion statements, statistics, research results, survey results). Create a master bibliography of the texts so that students can get their own copies of additional texts that interest them.

Writing Task: Think about the hot topic that you debated in class. What is your point of view on the subject? Write a blog entry in which you prove your point of view.

Writing Prompt 5

Context for Writing: Have the class research the question "Is college worth it?" Each student should bring in and report on at least one informational text that has solid evidence on the topic. Examples of solid evidence are statistics about tuition and debt, salaries for degreed and non-degreed workers, examples of successful people who did or did not get a college degree, or a psychologist's article on the value of individualized life goals. For example, success for one person might be completing cosmetology school or becoming a certified diesel mechanic instead of getting a bachelor's degree.

Writing Task: Is a college education necessary to a high-school graduate's success? Write an argument to convince your classmates of your point of view.

Checklist for Writing an Argument
Grades 11–12

Use this checklist to make sure you include the essential elements in the title, introduction, body, and conclusion of your argument.

Title. Give your paper a title that identifies the topic, hints at your claim (such as asking a rhetorical question), or expresses your claim outright. You might think of other ways to make your title informative *and* interesting.

Introductory Section. Introduce the debatable topic and state your claim (your judgment, point of view, or opinion). If your claim is about a work of literature or other text, give the title and author of the work. Introduce these key elements in the order that best highlights your claim. You might choose to introduce an opposing claim in this section or wait until the body of your paper.

Body Paragraphs. Develop your claim by explaining reasons and evidence that show your claim to be focused, logical, and defensible. Choose only the most convincing reasons, opting for quality over quantity, to create a strong argument. Likewise, develop the opposing viewpoint by explaining its limitations objectively (no insults or other logical fallacies). Show your understanding of the topic by choosing relevant (not random) facts, details, examples, and quotations to support your claim.

Writer's Craft. To link ideas, sentences, and paragraphs clearly, use words and phrases that signal comparisons, contrasts, a cause-and-effect relationship, sequence, or add ons. Some examples are *for instance*, *however*, *therefore*, *later*, and *moreover*. Use varied syntax in the construction of your sentences. In addition, use a formal writing style throughout the paper. Document direct quotations and paraphrased ideas using a formatting guide such as MLA.

Conclusion. In the conclusion statement or section, reinforce your claim with a final thought, a restatement of your claim, a summary of your strongest reasons, or a similar technique. Don't just repeat what you said in your introduction; provide insight into your claim based on the reasons you have shared.

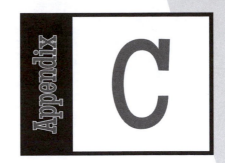

Blank Lesson Plan Template

Use the following template to create your own Common Core lesson plans in reading, writing, speaking/listening, and language. Remember that your lessons should be integrated when possible and cover more than one standard.

Common Core Lesson Plan

Topic/Title: _____

Grade Level:

Time Frame:

Overview:

Common Core State Standards

-
-
-
-

Objectives

-
-
-
-

Background Knowledge Required

Materials Needed

-
-
-
-

183

Agenda

1.

2.

3.

4.

5.

Extend the Lesson

- ▪

- ▪

Differentiation

For students who need extra support

- ▪

- ▪

For advanced students

- ▪

- ▪

Assessment

-
-
-
-

Additional Resources

-
-

Notes

After implementing the lesson, reflect on what worked and what you would change the next time.

_____

_____

_____

_____

References

Achenbach, J. (1996, December 4).The age of bad information. *The Washington Post*. Retrieved from www.washingtonpost.com/blogs/achenblog/post/archive-the-age-of-bad-information/2012/08/06/fb8bf1fe-dfc4-11e1-8fc5-a7dcf1fc161d_blog.html.

Benjamin, A., & Crow, J. T. (2013). *Vocabulary at the core: Teaching the Common Core standards*. Larchmont, NY: Eye On Education.

Blue, L. (2012). 6 ways to keep your pets safe in the heat. *Time.com: Healthland*. Retrieved from healthland.time.com/2012/08/03/6-ways-to-keep-your-pets-safe-in-the-heat/?iid=hl-article-special-reports-widget#know-the-signs-of-heatstroke

Calkins, L., Ehrenworth, M., & Lehman, C. (2012). *Pathways to the Common Core: Accelerating achievement*. Portsmouth, NH: Heinemann.

Coleman, D. & Pimentel, S. (2012). *Revised publishers' criteria for the Common Core State Standards in English language arts and literacy, grades 3–12*. Washington, D.C.: The National Association of State Boards of Education, Council of Chief State School Officers, Achieve, and the Council of the Great City Schools.

Kennedy, John F. (1963, June 11). Report to the American People on Civil Rights, 11 June 1963. Retrieved from www.jfklibrary.org/Asset-Viewer/LH8F_0Mzv0e6Ro1yEm74Ng.aspx

McCullers, C. (1988). A tree, a rock, a cloud. In A. S. Landy (Ed.), *The Heath introduction to literature* (3rd ed.) (pp. 390–396). Lexington, MA: D. C. Heath and Company.

Mohr, N. (1993). A time with a future (Carmela). In R. Barreca (Ed.), *Women of the century: Thirty modern short stories* (p. 289). New York, NY: St. Martin's Press.

National Governors Association Center for Best Practices, Council of Chief State School Officers (2010). *Common Core State Standards for English language arts*. Washington, D.C.: National Governors Association Center for Best Practices, Council of Chief State School Officers. Retrieved from www.corestandards.org/the-standards.

Sacks, O. (1985). *The man who mistook his wife for a hat and other clinical tales*. New York, NY: Harper and Row.

Sifferlin, A. (2012). Stick to Sesame Street: Violent TV disrupts kids' sleep. *Time.com: Healthland*. Retrieved from healthland.time.com/2012/08/06/stick-to-sesame-street-violent-tv-disrupts-kids-sleep/?iid=hl-article-mostpop1

Zinsser, W. (1998). *On writing well*. New York, NY: HarperCollins Publishers.

Notes